HOW TO SELL LIKE CRAZY ON FACEBOOK MARKETPLACE

CREATING AN UNCONTESTED MARKETPLACE ON FACEBOOK, STRATEGIC LEAD GENERATION, BUILDING A NEW CUSTOMER BASE, AND ESTABLISHING PRODUCT DOMINANCE.

Dr. Lucas Anderson

Content

Introduction

Welcome to the world of Facebook Marketplace, a thriving ecosystem where everyday sellers like yourself have the opportunity to make fortunes. I'm Dr. Lucas Anderson, and for years I've been immersed in the world of online selling. Through my expertise, I've helped countless clients achieve remarkable success on Facebook Marketplace, transforming their businesses and their lives in the process.

In "How to Sell Like Crazy on Facebook Marketplace," I'm excited to share with you the strategies, tactics, and insider secrets that have propelled my clients to incredible heights of success. From small-time sellers turning a hobby into a thriving business to established entrepreneurs expanding their reach, the potential on Facebook Marketplace is limitless.

The Power of Facebook Marketplace

Let's talk about the power of Facebook Marketplace. With over a billion active users, this platform is a goldmine waiting to be tapped. Imagine having access to a massive audience, all eager to discover what you have to offer. It's not just about numbers—it's about the opportunity to connect with buyers in your local community and beyond, all without spending a dime on listing fees.

I've seen my clients go from struggling to find buyers for their products to selling out within hours of listing on Facebook Marketplace. The platform's integration into the Facebook app means that your listings are not just static posts—they're part of a dynamic, engaging environment where buyers are actively looking for what you have to offer.

Why This Book Matters

So why am I sharing these strategies with you? Because I've witnessed firsthand the incredible impact they can have. My clients have gone from side hustles to full-time businesses, from financial stress to financial freedom. These strategies have helped them make fortunes, and I want the same for you.

In "How to Sell Like Crazy on Facebook Marketplace," you'll discover the exact steps my clients have taken to achieve their success. Whether you're looking to declutter your home, start a part-time gig, or scale your existing business, the strategies in this book are your roadmap to achieving your goals.

What to Expect

Throughout the following chapters, I'll be sharing the proven methods that have worked time and time again. We'll start by diving into creating an uncontested marketplace, where you'll learn how to identify untapped niches and position your products for maximum success. From there, we'll explore strategic lead generation techniques, building a loyal customer base, and establishing dominance in your market.

You'll hear real stories of clients who have turned a simple idea into a six-figure business using Facebook Marketplace. These success stories aren't just luck—they're the result of strategic planning, targeted marketing, and a deep understanding of how to leverage this platform to its fullest potential.

So, whether you're a seasoned seller looking to take your business to the next level or a newcomer eager to get started, this book is your comprehensive guide to achieving success on Facebook Marketplace. Get ready to unlock the power of this platform and start selling like crazy!

Let's dive in and make your fortune on Facebook Marketplace.

Chapter One

Understanding Facebook Marketplace

Welcome to the world of Facebook Marketplace, a digital marketplace where opportunities abound for savvy sellers. In this chapter, we'll explore the intricacies of Facebook Marketplace, uncovering its vast potential and the myriad benefits it offers to sellers of all kinds.

Introduction to Facebook Marketplace

Facebook Marketplace isn't just another online selling platform—it's a dynamic marketplace integrated directly into the world's largest social network. With over 2 billion active users on Facebook, the potential reach of your listings is immense. This means that whether you're selling handmade crafts, vintage treasures, or brand-new electronics, there's a highly engaged audience waiting to discover what you have to offer.

Unlike traditional e-commerce platforms, Facebook Marketplace is inherently social. This social aspect is a powerful driver of engagement, as users can easily share listings with friends, comment on items they like, and even see when mutual friends are interested in a product. This social proof can be invaluable for sellers, as it adds a layer of credibility and trust to their listings.

Benefits of Selling on Facebook

Zero Listing Fees: One of the most attractive aspects of Facebook Marketplace is that it's entirely free to use. There are no listing fees or commission charges, which means you can showcase your products without any upfront costs eating into your profits.

Massive Audience: With billions of users scrolling through their Facebook feeds every day, your listings have the potential to reach a vast audience. Whether you're targeting local buyers or a broader market, the sheer number of active users ensures that your products will get visibility.

Localized Selling: Facebook Marketplace is designed for local selling, making it ideal for buyers and sellers looking for convenient, in-person transactions. Buyers can filter their searches by location, ensuring that they find products available in their area. This localized approach is particularly beneficial for sellers of bulky or heavy items that are impractical to ship.

Integration with Messenger: Communication is seamless on Facebook Marketplace, thanks to its integration with Messenger. Buyers can message sellers directly with questions, requests for additional photos, or to arrange a meeting. This instant communication fosters trust and can lead to quicker sales.

Overview of Facebook Marketplace Features

Now, let's take a closer look at some of the key features that make Facebook Marketplace a powerful selling tool:

Listing Creation: Creating a listing on Facebook Marketplace is a straightforward process. You can upload multiple photos of your item, write a detailed description, set a price, and specify your location. High-quality photos and a compelling description can significantly increase the chances of your item selling.

Categories and Filters: To help buyers find what they're looking for, Facebook Marketplace offers a range of categories and filters. Whether someone is searching for clothing, electronics, furniture, or vehicles, they can easily narrow down their options.

Saved Searches: Buyers can save searches for specific items, allowing them to receive notifications when new listings matching their criteria are posted. As a seller, this means that your listings may be seen by interested buyers shortly after you post them.

Shipping Options: While Facebook Marketplace primarily focuses on local transactions, it also offers shipping options for certain items. Sellers can choose to offer shipping and set shipping costs, expanding their potential customer base beyond their immediate area.

Reviews and Ratings: Sellers and buyers on Facebook Marketplace can leave reviews and ratings based on their transactions. Positive reviews can boost your credibility as a seller and encourage others to trust your listings.

Navigating Marketplace: A Step-by-Step Guide

Let me walk you through the process of navigating Facebook Marketplace to help you get started:

Accessing Marketplace: To access Facebook Marketplace, open the Facebook app on your mobile device or visit the Facebook website on your computer. Look for the

Marketplace icon, which typically appears as a storefront icon at the bottom of the app or on the left-hand sidebar on the website.

Exploring Categories: Once you're in Marketplace, you'll find a variety of categories to explore. These categories range from Home and Garden to Electronics, Vehicles, Clothing, and more. Click on a category to see listings related to that category.

Searching for Items: If you're looking for something specific, use the search bar at the top of the Marketplace page. Enter keywords related to the item you're seeking, such as "vintage furniture" or "iPhone X," and hit enter. You can also use filters to narrow down your search by location, price range, condition, and more.

Viewing Listings: When you find a listing that catches your eye, click on it to view more details. Here, you'll see photos of the item, a description provided by the seller, the price, the seller's location, and any shipping options available.

Contacting Sellers: If you have questions about an item or would like to negotiate the price, you can easily message the seller. Simply click on the "Message" button on the listing, and a chat window will open in Messenger. Here, you can communicate with the seller directly, ask questions, and arrange a meeting if needed.

Creating Your Own Listing: Ready to start selling? Click on the "Sell Something" button on the Marketplace homepage. You'll be prompted to upload photos of your item, write a compelling description, set a price, and select a category. Be sure to provide as much detail as possible to attract potential buyers.

By following these steps, you'll be well on your way to navigating Facebook Marketplace like a pro.

Case Study:

Meet Maria: From Local Artisan to Online Success with Facebook Marketplace.

Meet Maria. She's a talented jewelry maker with a passion for creating unique, handcrafted pieces. For years, Maria had been selling her jewelry at local craft fairs and through word-of-mouth referrals. While she loved what she did, she often found herself wishing for a larger audience to showcase her creations to.

One day, Maria reached out to me for advice on expanding her jewelry business. She was eager to take her craft to the next level but wasn't sure where to start. That's when I introduced her to the world of Facebook Marketplace.

"Maria," I said, "have you ever considered selling your jewelry on Facebook Marketplace? It's a powerful platform with millions of active users, and I think it could be the perfect place for you to reach a broader audience."

Maria was intrigued but also a bit hesitant. She had never ventured into online selling before and wasn't sure how to navigate the digital landscape. That's where my expertise came in.

Together, we sat down and I guided her through the process of setting up her first listing on Facebook Marketplace. We took beautiful photos of her jewelry, highlighting the intricate details and vibrant colors. I helped her craft a compelling description that showcased the passion and care she put into each piece.

As we uploaded the listing, I explained to Maria the potential reach of Facebook Marketplace. "Maria, think of this as your virtual storefront," I said. "Instead of waiting for customers to come to you, you're putting your jewelry right in front of them, where they're already scrolling and looking for treasures."

Within hours of posting her first listing, Maria received her first message from a potential buyer. Excitement filled her as she responded, answering questions and providing more information about her jewelry. Soon enough, she made her first sale.

But the magic didn't stop there. Word started to spread among Maria's friends and family. They shared her listings on their own Facebook pages, tagging friends who they thought would love her jewelry. Maria's creations were suddenly reaching far beyond her local community, attracting buyers from different cities and even states.

As the weeks went by, Maria's business boomed. Her once modest hobby had transformed into a thriving online jewelry store. She was selling out of pieces faster than she could make them, and her inbox was filled with messages from satisfied customers praising her craftsmanship.

"It's incredible," Maria said to me one day, her eyes shining with excitement. "I never imagined that Facebook Marketplace would open up this world of opportunities for me. It's not just about selling my jewelry—it's about connecting with people who appreciate what I do."

Maria's success story is just one of many that I've had the privilege to witness. Through my expertise and guidance, I've helped countless clients like Maria discover the wonders and potentials of Facebook Marketplace. Whether you're a jewelry maker, a vintage collector, or a tech enthusiast, this platform offers a gateway to reach a vast audience and turn your passion into profits.

Going forward, we'll explore the strategies and techniques that have helped Maria and others like her achieve success on Facebook Marketplace. From creating compelling listings to building a loyal customer base, we'll cover it all. Get ready to embark on a journey that could transform your business and open doors to new possibilities. Let's dive in and uncover the power of Facebook Marketplace together.

This is what I do and I have a lot of secret to share with you in this book.

Learn what I teach you and implement them that's exactly what Maria and many other clients did to change their stories.

Chapter Two

Creating an Uncontested Marketplace

We're going to explore the art of creating an uncontested marketplace on Facebook. This is where the magic happens. Where you carve out your niche, position your products strategically, and set yourself apart from the competition. Get ready to discover how to make your marketplace presence stand out like never before.

Identifying Niche Markets

The first step in creating an uncontested marketplace is identifying your niche. What sets your products apart? What unique value do they offer? Take some time to think about who your ideal customer is and what problem your product solves for them.

Let's take an example from one of my clients called Sarah, a talented artist who creates stunning hand-painted ceramics. Instead of simply listing her ceramics as "hand-painted ceramics," Sarah identifies a niche within her market based the advice I gave her. She specializes in creating personalized pet-themed ceramics, targeting pet owners who want a unique and special way to celebrate their furry friends.

By narrowing her focus to a specific niche, Sarah makes her products more appealing to a targeted audience. Instead of trying to appeal to everyone, she's speaking directly to pet lovers who are looking for something special and personalized.

Conducting Market Research

Once you've identified your niche, it's time to dive into market research. This step is crucial for understanding your audience, analyzing competitors, and identifying trends.

Start by exploring Facebook Marketplace itself. Look at similar listings in your niche to get a sense of pricing, descriptions, and photos. Pay attention to what's working well for other sellers and where there may be gaps or opportunities for improvement.

Outside of Facebook Marketplace, use tools like Google Trends, industry reports, and social media insights to gather data. Are there emerging trends in your niche? What are customers talking about on social media? The more you understand your market, the better equipped you'll be to position your products effectively.

Positioning Your Products for Success

With your niche identified and market research completed, it's time to position your products for success. This involves several key elements:

Unique Selling Proposition (USP): What makes your products unique? This could be the quality of materials, your craftsmanship, customization options, or something else entirely. Clearly communicate your USP in your listings to grab buyers' attention.

Compelling Descriptions: Use descriptive language that paints a picture for potential buyers. Instead of just listing features, tell a story. For example, instead of saying "hand-painted ceramics," Sarah might describe her products as "custom, one-of-a-kind ceramic art pieces, lovingly painted by hand to capture the unique personality of your beloved pet."

High-Quality Photos: Invest time in capturing high-quality photos of your products. Clear, well-lit images can make a world of difference in attracting buyers. For Sarah, this might mean taking photos of her ceramics with different angles and lighting to showcase the intricate details.

Pricing Strategy: Set your prices strategically. Consider your costs, market demand, and perceived value of your products. Sarah might price her personalized pet ceramics slightly higher than generic ceramics, emphasizing the added value of customization.

Setting Yourself Apart from Competitors

In a crowded marketplace, differentiation is key. Here are some strategies to set yourself apart from competitors:

Exceptional Customer Service: Go above and beyond to provide excellent customer service. Respond to messages promptly, address any concerns or questions, and ensure a smooth buying experience.

Create a Brand Story: Share the story behind your products. People love to connect with the human side of businesses. For Sarah, she might share how her love for animals inspired her to create personalized pet ceramics.

Offer Something Extra: Consider adding a bonus or special offer with purchases. This could be a handwritten thank-you note, a small gift, or a discount on their next purchase.

Engage with Your Community: Build a community around your brand. Share behind-the-scenes glimpses of your creative process, run contests or giveaways, and encourage customers to share photos of their purchases.

By implementing these strategies, you're not just selling products—you're creating an experience for your customers. You're positioning yourself as the go-to seller in your niche, offering something truly unique and valuable.

Putting It into Action

Now that you understand the importance of creating an uncontested marketplace, it's time to put these strategies into action. Take a look at your current listings and see how you can refine them to better target your niche. Experiment with different descriptions, photos, and pricing strategies to find what resonates best with your audience.

Remember, creating an uncontested marketplace is about more than just selling products—it's about creating a brand and a story that customers want to be a part of. As you continue on this journey, keep refining and adapting your approach based on feedback and results.

Now let take a closer look at real-life examples of sellers who have gone through my hands and have mastered the art of creating an uncontested marketplace on Facebook. These case studies will provide valuable insights and inspiration for how you can apply similar strategies to your own business.

Case Studies

Case Study 1: Sarah's Pet-themed Ceramics

Sarah, a talented artist, who had the passion for creating hand-painted ceramics. However, she noticed that the market for generic ceramics was saturated, with many sellers offering similar products. Determined to stand out, Sarah decided to use these strategies and focus on a niche market: personalized pet-themed ceramics.

Sarah realized that pet owners were always looking for unique ways to celebrate their beloved companions. By specializing in pet-themed ceramics, she tapped into a passionate and devoted audience.

Sarah spent time researching pet owners' preferences and trends in the pet industry. She studied popular pet breeds, colors, and styles that resonated with her target audience. This research helped her create designs that were not only aesthetically pleasing but also highly appealing to pet lovers.

Sarah's listings on Facebook Marketplace were not just about selling ceramics—they were about capturing the essence of each pet. Her descriptions were heartfelt and personal, highlighting the stories behind each piece. Sarah also invested in professional photography to showcase the intricate details of her work.

What set Sarah apart was her attention to detail and personalized touch. Each ceramic piece was custom-made to resemble the buyer's pet, complete with unique markings and features. This level of customization and care made her listings stand out in a sea of generic ceramics.

The result? Sarah's pet-themed ceramics quickly gained traction on Facebook Marketplace. Pet owners were thrilled to have a one-of-a-kind artwork that celebrated their furry friends. Word-of-mouth spread, and soon, Sarah's business was booming. She went from struggling to find buyers for her generic ceramics to having a loyal customer base of pet owners who couldn't get enough of her personalized creations.

Case Study 2: Alex's Eco-Friendly Home Goods

Alex was passionate about sustainability and eco-friendly living. He noticed a gap in the market for affordable, stylish, and environmentally conscious home goods. Armed with this insight, Alex set out to create an uncontested marketplace for his eco-friendly products.

Alex identified a growing trend among consumers who were seeking sustainable alternatives for everyday household items. He realized that there was a demand for products that were both eco-friendly and aesthetically pleasing.

Alex conducted extensive research on eco-friendly materials, manufacturing processes, and consumer preferences. He looked at what his competitors were offering and identified areas where he could differentiate his products.

Alex's listings on Facebook Marketplace emphasized the eco-friendly aspects of his products. He highlighted the materials used, such as bamboo, recycled glass, and organic cotton. His descriptions emphasized the benefits of choosing sustainable options for the home, from reducing plastic waste to supporting ethical manufacturing practices.

What made Alex's products unique was their combination of style and sustainability. While there were other eco-friendly options on the market, Alex's items stood out for their modern designs and affordability. He also offered tips on how customers could incorporate sustainable living into their homes, creating added value for his listings.

The response was overwhelming. Eco-conscious consumers flocked to Alex's listings, eager to support his mission of promoting sustainable living. His products gained a reputation for being both environmentally friendly and fashionable, appealing to a wide range of buyers who wanted to make a positive impact on the planet without sacrificing style.

Key Takeaways

These case studies illustrate the power of identifying niche markets, conducting thorough market research, positioning products strategically, and setting yourself apart from competitors. Whether it's through personalized ceramics or eco-friendly home goods, these sellers found success by tapping into the unique needs and desires of their target audiences.

As you consider your own Facebook Marketplace strategy, think about what sets your products apart. How can you create a niche market that is uncontested and highly appealing to your ideal customers? By following the examples of Sarah and Alex, you can craft listings that stand out, attract high-quality leads, and ultimately, turn them into loyal customers.

We'll delve into the world of strategic lead generation, exploring how to attract the right audience to your listings and convert them into sales. Get ready to learn the techniques that will help you build a thriving customer base on Facebook Marketplace!

Chapter Three

Strategic Lead Generation

In this chapter, we'll delve into the critical aspect of strategic lead generation on Facebook Marketplace. Effective lead generation is the lifeblood of any successful selling strategy—it's about attracting the right audience, engaging them with compelling listings, and ultimately converting them into loyal customers. Let's explore the key tactics and techniques to master this crucial aspect of selling like crazy on Facebook Marketplace.

The Importance of Targeted Advertising

Targeted advertising is a game-changer when it comes to lead generation on Facebook Marketplace. Instead of casting a wide net and hoping for the best, targeted advertising allows you to reach the specific audience most likely to be interested in your products. Using features like:

Custom Audiences: Facebook's Custom Audiences feature lets you target users based on their interests, behaviors, and demographics. For example, if you're selling fitness equipment, you can target users who have shown an interest in fitness-related pages or activities.

Lookalike Audiences: Lookalike Audiences are another powerful tool. These are audiences created by Facebook that resemble your existing customers. By targeting lookalike audiences, you're reaching users who share similar traits and interests with your current customer base.

Crafting Compelling Product Listings

Your product listings are your virtual storefront on Facebook Marketplace. To attract leads and entice them to click, it's crucial to create compelling and persuasive listings.

Clear and Descriptive Titles: Your title should grab attention and clearly convey what you're selling. Instead of "Handmade Soap," try "Luxurious Handcrafted Lavender Soap - Perfect for Relaxation."

High-Quality Photos: Invest time in capturing high-quality photos of your products. Clear, well-lit images that showcase the details will pique the interest of potential buyers.

Detailed Descriptions: Use your description to tell a story about your product. Highlight its features, benefits, and why it's a must-have. For example, if you're selling a handbag, describe the materials used, the craftsmanship, and how it can elevate an outfit.

Compelling Call-to-Action (CTA): Encourage users to take action with a clear CTA. Whether it's "Shop Now,"

"Learn More," or "Send Message for Details," make it easy for leads to engage with your listing.

Engagement Tactics to Attract Leads

Engagement is key to building trust and attracting leads on Facebook Marketplace. Here are some tactics to boost engagement:

Respond Promptly: When users comment or message you with inquiries, respond promptly and professionally. A quick response shows that you're attentive and customer-focused.

Encourage Reviews and Recommendations: Positive reviews and recommendations can go a long way in attracting leads. Encourage satisfied customers to leave feedback and showcase these testimonials on your page.

Run Contests or Giveaways: Contests and giveaways are excellent ways to generate buzz and attract leads.

Require participants to like your page or share your post to enter, increasing visibility.

Using Facebook Insights for Lead Generation

Facebook Insights provides valuable data about your audience, their preferences, and how they interact with your listings. Here's how to leverage this information for lead generation:

Audience Demographics: Use Insights to understand the demographics of your audience, such as age, gender, location, and interests. This helps you tailor your listings and targeting for maximum impact.

Post Engagement: Analyze which posts receive the most engagement. This can guide you in creating similar content that resonates with your audience and attracts leads.

Timing: Insights can reveal the times when your audience is most active. Schedule your posts and promotions during these peak times to reach a larger audience.

Optimizing Your Reach: Tips and Tricks

To further optimize your reach and attract leads, consider these additional tips and tricks:

Utilize Hashtags: Hashtags can increase the discoverability of your listings. Use relevant hashtags related to your products, such as #handmade, #vintage, or #ecofriendly.

Share User-Generated Content: If customers share photos or positive experiences with your products, repost this content on your page. It's authentic and can attract leads who see real people enjoying your offerings.

Promote Local Listings: If you're targeting local buyers, specify your location in your listings. Many users on Facebook Marketplace filter by location, so this can increase visibility for your products in your area.

Cross-Promote on Other Platforms: Share your Facebook Marketplace listings on other social media platforms, your website, or through email newsletters. This expands your reach and brings in leads from different channels.

Putting It into Action

Now that you've learned the strategies for strategic lead generation on Facebook Marketplace, it's time to put them into action. Review your current listings and see how you can optimize them for targeted advertising, engagement, and utilizing Facebook Insights.

Experiment with different tactics, track your results using Insights, and refine your approach based on what works best for your audience. By continuously optimizing your lead generation efforts, you'll attract high-quality leads, convert them into customers, and ultimately, achieve success on Facebook Marketplace.

In the next chapter, we'll delve into the world of building a new customer base, exploring how to turn leads into loyal customers who keep coming back for more. Get ready to learn the strategies that will help you build a thriving community around your products on Facebook Marketplace!

Chapter Four

Building a New Customer Base

Congratulations! You've attracted leads to your Facebook Marketplace listings. Now, it's time to focus on converting these leads into loyal customers. We'll explore the strategies and techniques to build a strong customer base that keeps coming back for more.

Converting Leads into Loyal Customers

Converting leads into loyal customers is the ultimate goal of any selling strategy. It's about building trust, providing value, and delivering exceptional experiences. Here's how you can do it:

Personalized Follow-Ups: After a lead expresses interest in your product, follow up with a personalized message. Address them by name, thank them for their interest, and offer any additional information they may need.

Special Offers: Provide exclusive offers or discounts to leads to incentivize them to make a purchase. Limited-time promotions or "first-purchase" discounts can create a sense of urgency and encourage conversion.

Showcase Customer Testimonials: Share testimonials and reviews from satisfied customers on your Facebook page. Seeing positive feedback from others can reassure leads and instill confidence in your products.

Effective Communication Strategies

Communication is key to building relationships with your customers. Here are some effective strategies:

Clear and Timely Responses: When a customer reaches out with questions or concerns, respond promptly and professionally. Clear communication builds trust and shows that you value their inquiries.

Use Messenger Wisely: Facebook Messenger is a powerful tool for communication. Use it to provide real-time support, answer product inquiries, and assist with the buying process.

Personalization: Tailor your messages to each customer's needs and preferences. Address them by name and reference their past interactions with your brand. Personalized communication makes customers feel valued and appreciated.

Providing Top-Notch Customer Service

Exceptional customer service is a cornerstone of building a loyal customer base. Here's how you can provide top-notch service:

Easy Return and Refund Policies: Make it simple for customers to return or exchange products if they're not satisfied. A hassle-free return policy shows that you stand behind your products.

Go Above and Beyond: Surprise and delight your customers with unexpected gestures. This could be a handwritten thank-you note with their purchase, a small freebie, or a discount on their next order.

Stay Professional and Courteous: Even if a customer is unhappy, maintain professionalism in your interactions. Address their concerns calmly and offer solutions to resolve any issues.

Post-Purchase Engagement Techniques

The relationship with your customers doesn't end after they make a purchase. Here's how to keep them engaged:

Follow-Up Emails: Send a follow-up email after a purchase to thank the customer, confirm their order, and provide any relevant information, such as tracking details.

Ask for Feedback: Encourage customers to leave reviews and feedback about their experience. Positive reviews not only build credibility but also attract more customers.

Share Relevant Content: Keep customers engaged with your brand by sharing relevant content on your Facebook page. This could include product updates, behind-the-scenes glimpses, or tips and tricks related to your products.

Exclusive Content and Offers: Reward loyal customers with exclusive content or offers. This could be sneak peeks of upcoming products, early access to sales, or VIP discounts.

Putting It into Action

Now that you have the strategies for building a new customer base, it's time to put them into action:

Create Automated Responses: Set up automated responses on Facebook Messenger to acknowledge messages and inquiries from customers.

Implement a Loyalty Program: Consider starting a loyalty program where customers earn points for purchases, referrals, or social media engagement.

Monitor Customer Feedback: Regularly check for customer feedback and reviews. Address any negative feedback promptly and use it as an opportunity to improve.

Engage on social media: Actively engage with customers on your Facebook page. Respond to comments, share user-generated content, and participate in conversations.

By focusing on converting leads into loyal customers, providing exceptional customer service, and engaging with customers even after the purchase, you'll build a customer base that keeps coming back for more.

we'll delve into real-life case studies of sellers who have successfully converted leads into loyal customers on Facebook Marketplace. These stories will showcase the power of effective communication, top-notch customer service, and post-purchase engagement in building a strong and loyal customer base.

Case Studies

Case Study 1: Emma's Handmade Jewelry

Emma, a talented jewelry maker, had been struggling to convert leads into customers for her handmade jewelry business. She had a strong presence on Facebook Marketplace, with beautifully crafted listings that showcased her unique designs. However, she found that many leads would express interest but then hesitate to make a purchase.

Determined to improve her conversion rate, Emma started sending personalized follow-up messages to leads who had shown interest in her jewelry. She would address them by name, thank them for their interest, and offer additional information about the pieces they were interested in. This personal touch made a significant difference, as leads felt valued and more inclined to make a purchase.

To incentivize leads to make a purchase, Emma started offering limited-time discounts and promotions. For example, she ran a "Weekend Special" where customers could get 15% off their order. This created a sense of urgency and encouraged leads to take action.

Emma also began sharing customer testimonials and photos of happy customers wearing her jewelry on her Facebook page. Seeing real people enjoying her creations added credibility and reassurance for potential buyers.

The results were impressive. Emma saw a significant increase in her conversion rate, with leads turning into loyal customers who returned for repeat purchases. By focusing on personalized follow-ups, special offers, and showcasing customer testimonials, Emma built a strong customer base that continued to grow.

Case Study 2: David's Vintage Collectibles

David had a passion for vintage collectibles and had been selling them on Facebook Marketplace for some time. While he had a steady stream of leads, he noticed that many would browse his listings but not make a purchase.

David realized that communication was key to converting leads into customers. He started engaging with leads more actively, responding promptly to messages and inquiries. He provided detailed information about the history and provenance of each collectible, sparking interest and creating a connection with potential buyers.

David went above and beyond to provide exceptional customer service. When a customer had a question about a particular item, he would not only answer the question but also offer additional insights and stories about the collectible. This personalized approach made customers feel valued and more inclined to make a purchase.

After a customer made a purchase, David didn't stop there. He followed up with a personalized thank-you email, expressing his gratitude for their purchase and providing information about upcoming collections. This post-purchase engagement kept customers engaged with his brand and encouraged them to return for future purchases.

The results were remarkable. David saw an increase in repeat customers, with many buyers becoming collectors of his vintage items. By focusing on effective communication, top-notch customer service, and post-purchase engagement, David built a loyal customer base that continued to grow over time.

Key Takeaways

These case studies highlight the importance of effective communication, personalized follow-ups, special offers, and top-notch customer service in converting leads into loyal customers on Facebook Marketplace. By implementing these strategies, sellers like Emma and David were able to build strong customer bases that kept coming back for more.

As you consider your own customer conversion strategy, think about how you can tailor your approach to your audience. What personalized touches can you add to your communication? What special offers or promotions can you offer to incentivize purchases? How can you engage with customers even after they've made a purchase?

We'll explore how to establish dominance in your market on Facebook Marketplace. We'll uncover advanced strategies for standing out from the competition, becoming a trusted authority in your niche, and dominating the marketplace. Get ready to take your selling game to the next level!

Chapter Five

Establishing Product Dominance

The strategies and techniques for establishing product dominance on Facebook Marketplace can't underrate in the game of sales. Building brand authority, fostering trust with buyers, encouraging repeat purchases, leveraging reviews and testimonials, and scaling your business are all essential components of becoming a dominant force in your market. Let's explore how you can achieve product dominance and stand out as a leader on Facebook Marketplace.

Building Brand Authority on Facebook Marketplace

Brand authority is crucial for establishing trust and credibility with buyers. Here's how you can build and showcase your brand authority:

Consistent Branding: Maintain consistent branding across all your listings and social media channels. This includes your logo, colors, and messaging. Consistency builds recognition and trust with buyers.

Share Your Story: Use your Facebook page to share the story behind your brand. What inspired you to start your business? What values do you stand for? Personal stories resonate with customers and humanize your brand.

Educational Content: Become a valuable resource for your audience by sharing educational content related to your products or industry. This could include how-to guides, tips and tricks, or product demonstrations. By providing valuable information, you position yourself as an authority in your niche.

Fostering Trust with Buyers

Trust is the foundation of a successful business. Here's how you can foster trust with buyers on Facebook Marketplace:

Transparent Policies: Clearly outline your policies regarding shipping, returns, and customer service on your Facebook page and listings. Transparency builds trust and reassures buyers that they can shop with confidence.

Prompt and Professional Communication: Respond to inquiries and messages promptly and professionally. Clear and timely communication shows that you care about your customers and their needs.

Quality Assurance: Ensure that your products are of high quality and accurately represented in your listings. Honesty and integrity in your product descriptions build trust with buyers.

Encouraging Repeat Purchases

Repeat purchases are a key indicator of customer satisfaction and loyalty. Here's how you can encourage customers to come back for more:

Loyalty Programs: Implement a loyalty program where customers earn points for every purchase. Offer rewards such as discounts or exclusive perks for loyal customers.

Personalized Recommendations: Use customer purchase history to offer personalized recommendations for future purchases. For example, if a customer bought a dress, you can suggest accessories that complement it.

Follow-Up Offers: After a customer makes a purchase, follow up with a special offer for their next purchase. This could be a discount code or a free gift with their next order.

Leveraging Reviews and Testimonials

Positive reviews and testimonials are powerful social proof that can influence buying decisions. Here's how you can leverage them:

Encourage Reviews: Prompt satisfied customers to leave reviews on your Facebook page or product listings. You can send a follow-up email after a purchase with a gentle request for feedback.

Feature Testimonials: Showcase customer testimonials and reviews prominently on your Facebook page and listings. Seeing positive experiences from other buyers builds trust with potential customers.

Strategies for Scaling Your Business

Once you've established a strong foundation, it's time to scale your business for growth. Here are some strategies:

Expand Your Product Line: Introduce new products or variations based on customer feedback and market trends. Diversifying your offerings can attract a broader audience.

Optimize Operations: Streamline your processes for efficiency, from order fulfillment to customer service. This ensures a smooth experience for customers and allows you to handle increased demand.

Invest in Marketing: Allocate resources to marketing efforts that have proven effective, whether it's targeted advertising, influencer partnerships, or content marketing. A strategic marketing plan can help you reach a larger audience and drive sales.

Explore Partnerships: Consider partnering with complementary brands or influencers to expand your reach. Collaborations can introduce your products to new audiences and create buzz around your brand.

Putting It into Action

Now that you have the strategies for establishing product dominance on Facebook Marketplace, it's time to put them into action:

Audit Your Branding: Review your branding across all channels and ensure consistency. Update your Facebook page with compelling imagery and an engaging About section.

Share Your Story: Craft a compelling brand story to share with your audience. What makes your brand unique? Why should customers choose you? Share this story on your Facebook page and in your listings.

Implement Trust-building Measures: Review your policies and communication practices to ensure they inspire trust. Consider adding a dedicated FAQ section to address common questions from buyers.

Launch a Loyalty Program: If you haven't already, consider launching a loyalty program to reward repeat customers. Set up a system to track points and communicate program benefits to your audience.

Request and Showcase Reviews: Reach out to satisfied customers and request reviews. Feature these reviews prominently on your Facebook page and listings to build social proof.

Plan for Growth: Develop a growth strategy that includes expanding your product line, optimizing operations, investing in marketing, and exploring potential partnerships. Set clear goals and timelines for each initiative.

By following these strategies and taking actionable steps, you can establish product dominance on Facebook Marketplace and become a trusted authority in your niche.

We'll explore advanced techniques for maximizing your reach and growing your business even further. Get ready to take your Facebook Marketplace presence to new heights!

Chapter Six

Maximizing Sales with Advanced Techniques

We'll dive into advanced techniques for maximizing your sales on Facebook Marketplace. These strategies go beyond the basics and are designed to help you take your selling game to the next level. From cross-promotion strategies to running limited-time offers, leveraging Facebook groups, collaborations, and partnerships, to advanced tips for increasing sales, we'll cover it all.

Cross-Promotion Strategies

Cross-promotion is a powerful technique to expand your reach and attract new customers. Here's how you can implement cross-promotion strategies effectively:

Partner with Complementary Businesses: Identify businesses or sellers whose products complement yours. For example, if you sell handmade candles, you could partner with a seller of bath products. Cross-promote each other's products to reach a broader audience.

Bundle Deals: Create bundle deals where customers can purchase related products together at a discounted price. This encourages customers to buy more items from you while saving money.

Share on social media: Cross-promote your Facebook Marketplace listings on your other social media platforms, such as Instagram, Twitter, or Pinterest. Encourage followers to visit your Facebook page and check out your offerings.

Running Limited-Time Offers and Sales

Creating a sense of urgency can drive sales and motivate buyers to make a purchase. Here's how you can use limited-time offers and sales effectively:

Flash Sales: Offer short-term discounts or promotions for a few hours or a day. Promote these sales on your Facebook page and other channels to create buzz and urgency.

Holiday and Seasonal Promotions: Capitalize on holidays and seasonal events by offering special promotions. For example, offer a "Valentine's Day Sale" or a "Spring Cleaning Discount" to align with the season.

Create Exclusivity: Offer exclusive deals or early access to sales for your Facebook followers. This makes them feel special and encourages engagement with your page.

Leveraging Facebook Groups and Communities

Facebook Groups can be valuable resources for reaching a targeted audience and building relationships with potential customers. Here's how you can leverage Facebook Groups effectively:

Join Relevant Groups: Find and join groups that are relevant to your niche or target audience. Participate in discussions, provide valuable insights, and subtly promote your products when relevant.

Create Your Own Group: Consider creating a Facebook Group dedicated to your brand or products. This allows you to build a community around your brand, engage with customers directly, and share exclusive offers.

Collaborate with Group Admins: Build relationships with group admins and moderators. They can help promote your products within their groups, reaching a larger and more targeted audience.

Collaborations and Partnerships

Collaborating with other businesses or influencers can significantly expand your reach and credibility. Here's how you can approach collaborations:

Influencer Partnerships: Identify influencers or bloggers in your niche with a significant following. Collaborate with them to promote your products to their audience through sponsored posts, reviews, or giveaways.

Cross-Promotion with Brands: Partner with complementary brands for joint promotions or giveaways. This allows you to tap into each other's audiences and create excitement around your products.

Affiliate Programs: Create an affiliate program where influencers or partners earn a commission for every sale they drive to your listings. This incentivizes them to promote your products.

Advanced Tips for Increasing Sales

A/B Testing: Experiment with different listing titles, descriptions, and images to see what resonates best with your audience. Use A/B testing to compare the performance of different variations.

Optimize for Mobile: Ensure that your listings are mobile-friendly, as many users browse and shop on Facebook Marketplace from their smartphones. Use high-quality images and clear, concise descriptions that are easy to read on mobile devices.

Monitor Trends: Stay updated on industry trends and popular products. Offer trending items or create listings that align with current demand.

Upselling and Cross-Selling: When a customer is about to complete a purchase, suggest related or complementary products. This can increase the average order value and encourage additional purchases.

Putting It into Action

Create a Cross-Promotion Plan: Identify potential partners or businesses for cross-promotion. Reach out to them with collaboration ideas and create a schedule for promoting each other's products.

Plan Limited-Time Offers: Decide on the timing and details of your limited-time offers and sales. Create engaging graphics and promotional posts to generate excitement.

Engage in Facebook Groups: Join relevant Facebook Groups and start engaging with members. Share valuable insights, answer questions, and subtly promote your products when appropriate.

Explore Collaborations: Reach out to influencers or brands for potential collaborations. Pitch your ideas and discuss how you can work together to mutual benefit.

Implement Advanced Sales Techniques: Experiment with A/B testing, optimize your listings for mobile, and explore upselling and cross-selling opportunities.

By implementing these advanced techniques, you can maximize your sales on Facebook Marketplace and take your business to new heights. In the next chapter, we'll conclude our journey with key takeaways and a roadmap for continued success.

Chapter Seven

Overcoming Challenges and Pitfalls

Navigating the world of Facebook Marketplace comes with its own set of challenges. In this chapter, we'll explore common hurdles that sellers face and provide strategies for overcoming them. From dealing with competition and handling customer disputes to managing inventory, avoiding scams, and staying compliant with Facebook policies, we'll cover essential tips to help you navigate these challenges successfully.

Dealing with Competition

Competition on Facebook Marketplace can be fierce, but it's also an opportunity to differentiate yourself and stand out. Here's how you can navigate competition effectively:

Unique Selling Proposition (USP): Identify what sets your products apart from competitors. Whether it's superior quality, unique designs, or exceptional customer service, emphasize your USP in your listings and marketing.

Monitor Competitor Activity: Keep an eye on what your competitors are doing. Are they running promotions? Introducing new products? Use this information to adjust your strategies and stay competitive.

Focus on Customer Experience: Providing an excellent customer experience can set you apart. Offer personalized service, quick responses to inquiries, and hassle-free returns. Happy customers are more likely to return, regardless of competition.

Handling Customer Disputes and Returns

Despite your best efforts, there may be times when customers are unhappy with their purchases. Here's how to handle disputes and returns effectively:

Clear Policies: Have clear and concise policies regarding returns, refunds, and exchanges. Display these prominently on your Facebook page and listings.

Professional Communication: When a customer has an issue, respond promptly and professionally. Listen to their concerns, offer solutions, and strive to resolve the issue amicably.

Process for Returns: Have a streamlined process for handling returns. Provide instructions on how customers can initiate a return and what to expect throughout the process.

Managing Inventory and Fulfillment

Efficient inventory management and order fulfillment are essential for a smooth selling experience. Here are some tips:

Inventory Tracking: Use inventory management tools or spreadsheets to track your stock levels. This helps prevent overselling and ensures you have accurate information on hand.

Streamlined Fulfillment: Develop a process for quickly and accurately fulfilling orders. Label packages clearly, use reliable shipping methods, and provide tracking information to customers.

Anticipate Demand: Monitor trends and seasonal fluctuations to anticipate demand for certain products. This allows you to adjust your inventory and marketing strategies accordingly.

Avoiding Scams and Fraud

While most transactions on Facebook Marketplace are legitimate, it's essential to be cautious of potential scams and fraud. Here's how to protect yourself:

Verify Buyers: Before completing a sale, verify the buyer's identity and legitimacy. Check their profile, reviews, and any mutual connections.

Use Secure Payment Methods: Encourage buyers to use secure payment methods offered by Facebook, such as Facebook Pay. Avoid accepting payments through unofficial channels to prevent fraud.

Meet in Safe Locations: If meeting in person for a transaction, choose a public and well-lit location. Avoid isolated areas and always prioritize safety.

Staying Compliant with Facebook Policies

Facebook has specific policies and guidelines for Marketplace sellers. It's crucial to stay compliant to avoid penalties or account restrictions. Here's how:

Read and Understand Policies: Familiarize yourself with Facebook's Commerce Policies and Community Standards. Ensure your listings and activities adhere to these guidelines.

Authentic Listings: Only sell items that are authentic and accurately represented. Avoid selling prohibited items, such as weapons, drugs, or counterfeit goods.

Respect Community Guidelines: Engage with the Facebook Marketplace community respectfully. Avoid spamming, misleading claims, or inappropriate content.

Putting It into Action

Review and Update Policies: Take time to review your return, refund, and exchange policies. Ensure they are clear, fair, and prominently displayed.

Implement Inventory Management: If you haven't already, set up an inventory management system to track your stock levels and prevent overselling.

Stay Informed: Regularly review Facebook's Commerce Policies and Community Standards. Stay updated on any changes or updates that may affect your listings.

Educate Yourself: Take advantage of resources and guides provided by Facebook for Marketplace sellers. These can help you understand best practices and avoid pitfalls.

Monitor Activity: Keep an eye on your listings and interactions. Promptly address any potential issues, such as suspicious buyers or policy violations.

By proactively addressing these challenges and implementing strategies to overcome them, you can navigate the complexities of Facebook Marketplace with confidence. In the final chapter, we'll summarize key takeaways and provide a roadmap for continued success on Facebook Marketplace. Let's ensure your journey to selling like crazy is a successful one!

Chapter Eight

Future Trends and Innovations

As we look ahead to the future of Facebook Marketplace, it's essential to stay ahead of the curve and anticipate the evolving landscape of e-commerce. In this chapter, we'll explore the trends and innovations shaping the future of Marketplace selling, provide predictions for what's to come, and discuss how you can prepare your business for future success. Let's dive into the exciting world of e-commerce and Marketplace innovations.

The Evolving Landscape of Facebook Marketplace

Facebook Marketplace has undergone significant growth and transformation since its inception. From a platform for peer-to-peer selling to a robust e-commerce marketplace, it continues to evolve. Here are some key trends shaping its landscape:

Integration with Social Commerce: Expect to see tighter integration between Facebook Marketplace and other social media platforms. This will enable seamless shopping experiences directly from social posts and stories.

AI and Personalization: Artificial Intelligence (AI) will play a more significant role in Marketplace, providing personalized product recommendations based on user behavior and preferences.

Augmented Reality (AR): AR technology will enhance the shopping experience on Marketplace, allowing users to virtually try on clothing, preview furniture in their homes, and more.

Expansion of Categories: Marketplace will likely expand its categories beyond traditional goods to include services, rentals, and digital products.

Predictions for Future Trends

Based on current trends and emerging technologies, here are some predictions for the future of Facebook Marketplace:

Voice Commerce: With the rise of voice assistants like Siri and Alexa, voice commerce will become more prevalent. Users will be able to search for and purchase products using voice commands.

Sustainable and Ethical Shopping: As consumers become more environmentally conscious, there will be a growing demand for sustainable and ethically sourced products. Marketplace sellers who align with these values will have a competitive edge.

Social Shopping Experiences: Expect to see more interactive and social shopping experiences on Marketplace.

This could include live shopping events, group buying options, and virtual shopping parties.

Blockchain and Cryptocurrency: Blockchain technology may find its way into e-commerce, offering secure and transparent transactions. Cryptocurrency payments could become more common on Marketplace.

Preparing Your Business for Future Success

To thrive in the future of Facebook Marketplace, it's essential to adapt and innovate. Here's how you can prepare your business for future success:

Stay Agile and Adaptable: The e-commerce landscape is constantly changing. Stay informed about emerging trends and technologies, and be ready to pivot your strategies accordingly.

Invest in Technology: Consider investing in AI-powered tools for personalization, AR technology for immersive shopping experiences, and secure payment systems for cryptocurrency transactions.

Embrace Sustainability: If feasible for your business, explore ways to incorporate sustainability into your products and operations. This could include eco-friendly packaging, sourcing ethical materials, or supporting causes aligned with your brand values.

Build a Strong Online Presence: As competition grows, a strong online presence is crucial. Invest in high-quality product photography, engaging social media content, and customer reviews and testimonials.

Innovations in E-Commerce and Marketplace Selling

E-commerce as a whole is undergoing rapid innovation. Here are some innovations that could impact Marketplace selling:

Social Commerce: The convergence of social media and e-commerce will continue to grow. Look for opportunities to leverage social platforms for selling, such as Instagram Shops and Pinterest Buyable Pins.

Subscription Services: Subscription-based models offer recurring revenue and loyal customer bases. Consider offering subscription options for your products on Marketplace.

AI-Powered Customer Service: AI chatbots and virtual assistants can provide instant customer support and streamline the buying process.

Mobile Commerce: With the rise of mobile shopping, optimizing your listings and website for mobile devices is essential. Ensure a seamless and intuitive mobile shopping experience for customers.

Putting It into Action

Conduct Market Research: Stay informed about industry trends and consumer preferences. Monitor the latest innovations in e-commerce and Marketplace selling.

Invest in Training and Education: As new technologies emerge, invest in training for yourself and your team. Stay ahead of the curve with courses on AI, AR, and blockchain.

Stay Connected: Engage with the e-commerce community, attend industry conferences, and network with other sellers. Collaboration and knowledge-sharing can spark new ideas for your business.

Update Your Business Strategy: Regularly review and update your business strategy to align with future trends.

Be willing to experiment with new technologies and approaches.

By preparing your business for the future of Facebook Marketplace and embracing emerging trends and innovations, you can position yourself for continued success in the dynamic world of e-commerce. As we conclude this journey, remember that adaptability and innovation are key to thriving in the ever-changing marketplace landscape. Here's to your continued success as a seller on Facebook Marketplace!

Chapter Nine

Harnessing the Power of Data Analytics

In the digital age, data is king. As a Facebook Marketplace seller, leveraging data analytics can provide invaluable insights into customer behavior, trends, and opportunities for growth. In this chapter, we'll explore how you can harness the power of data analytics to make informed decisions, optimize your listings, and drive sales on Facebook Marketplace.

Understanding Your Metrics

The first step in harnessing data analytics is understanding the metrics that matter most to your business. Here are some key metrics to focus on:

Impressions and Reach: These metrics indicate how many users have seen your listings. A high number of impressions shows that your listings are being viewed by a wide audience.

Engagement: Engagement metrics such as likes, comments, and shares show how users are interacting with your listings. High engagement indicates that your listings are resonating with your audience.

Conversion Rate: The conversion rate measures the percentage of users who take a desired action, such as making a purchase, after viewing your listings. A high conversion rate indicates that your listings are effective in driving sales.

Customer Lifetime Value (CLV): CLV measures the total revenue a customer is expected to generate over their lifetime. Understanding CLV can help you tailor your marketing and customer retention strategies.

Optimizing Your Listings

Data analytics can help you optimize your listings for maximum effectiveness. Here's how:

A/B Testing: Experiment with different listing titles, descriptions, and images to see what performs best. A/B testing allows you to make data-driven decisions about what resonates most with your audience.

Keyword Optimization: Analyze keywords that are driving traffic to your listings and incorporate them strategically. This can improve your listings' visibility in search results.

Pricing Strategies: Use data to analyze pricing trends and competitor pricing. Adjust your pricing strategy based on data to stay competitive and maximize sales.

Personalizing the Customer Experience

Data analytics enables you to personalize the customer experience, creating a tailored journey for each customer. Here's how:

Recommendation Engines: Implement recommendation engines based on customer preferences and purchase history. This can increase cross-selling and upselling opportunities.

Personalized Emails: Use data to send personalized emails to customers based on their browsing and purchase history. This can include product recommendations, exclusive offers, and relevant content.

Segmentation: Segment your customer base based on demographics, purchase history, or behavior. This allows you to create targeted marketing campaigns that resonate with specific customer groups.

Identifying Trends and Opportunities

Data analytics can uncover trends and opportunities that you may not have otherwise noticed. Here's how to identify and capitalize on them:

Market Trends: Analyze data to identify emerging market trends and adjust your product offerings accordingly. This allows you to stay ahead of the curve and meet evolving customer demands.

Seasonal Trends: Use data to predict seasonal trends and adjust your inventory and marketing strategies accordingly. For example, if a particular product category tends to sell well during the holidays, you can stock up in advance.

Geographical Insights: Analyze data to understand where your customers are located. This can help you tailor your marketing efforts to specific geographic regions and optimize shipping and delivery options.

Tools and Resources for Data Analytics

There are a variety of tools and resources available to help you harness the power of data analytics:

Facebook Analytics: Utilize Facebook's built-in analytics tools to gain insights into your Marketplace performance. Monitor key metrics, track user behavior, and optimize your listings.

Google Analytics: If you have a website linked to your Facebook Marketplace listings, Google Analytics can provide valuable data on website traffic, user behavior, and conversion rates.

Third-Party Analytics Tools: Explore third-party analytics tools that are designed specifically for e-commerce sellers. These tools often offer advanced features for tracking and analyzing data.

Putting It into Action

Set Up Tracking: Ensure that you have tracking mechanisms in place to collect data on your Marketplace listings. This may involve setting up Facebook Pixel or other tracking tools.

Analyze and Interpret: Regularly analyze your data to uncover insights and trends. Look for patterns in customer behavior, popular products, and areas for improvement.

Optimize Listings: Use your data analysis to optimize your listings for maximum effectiveness. This may involve updating titles, descriptions, images, and pricing based on insights from your data.

Personalize Marketing: Implement personalized marketing strategies based on your customer data. Send targeted emails, create custom offers, and tailor your messaging to different customer segments.

Stay Agile: The e-commerce landscape is dynamic, so be prepared to adapt your strategies based on data insights.

Continuously monitor and adjust your approach to stay competitive.

By harnessing the power of data analytics, you can gain valuable insights into your customers, optimize your listings, and capitalize on emerging trends and opportunities. In the next chapter, we'll delve into the importance of customer feedback and how you can use it to improve your business on Facebook Marketplace. Let's continue to elevate your selling game with actionable insights and strategies!

Chapter Ten

Connecting the Power of social media for Marketplace Success

In the digital age, social media has become an indispensable tool for businesses, offering unparalleled opportunities for reaching and engaging with customers. In this chapter, we'll explore how you can harness the power of social media to elevate your success on Facebook Marketplace. From building a strong brand presence to leveraging social media marketing strategies, we'll delve into the tactics that can drive traffic, increase sales, and foster customer loyalty.

Building a Strong Brand Presence

Your brand's presence on social media is an extension of your identity on Facebook Marketplace. Here's how you can build a strong brand presence:

Consistent Branding: Ensure that your brand's visual identity, such as logos, colors, and imagery, remains consistent across all social media platforms. Consistency fosters recognition and trust among your audience.

Compelling Content: Create engaging and relevant content that resonates with your target audience. This could include product showcases, behind-the-scenes glimpses, customer testimonials, and industry insights.

Interactive Posts: Encourage interaction with your audience through polls, contests, and interactive stories. This not only boosts engagement but also helps you gather valuable feedback.

Leveraging Social Media Marketing Strategies

Social media offers a plethora of marketing tools and strategies to amplify your presence and drive sales. Here are some effective strategies to consider:

Targeted Advertising: Utilize Facebook's powerful advertising platform to target specific demographics, interests, and behaviors. Create compelling ad creatives and monitor performance to optimize results.

Influencer Collaborations: Partner with influencers or micro-influencers in your niche to reach their engaged audience. Influencers can showcase your products authentically and drive traffic to your Marketplace listings.

Hashtag Campaigns: Create branded hashtags and encourage customers to use them when sharing their purchases or experiences. This builds a community around your brand and increases visibility.

Live Shopping Events: Host live shopping events on platforms like Facebook Live or Instagram Live. Showcase your products in real-time, answer questions, and offer exclusive deals for viewers.

Engaging with Your Audience

Social media is not just about broadcasting messages; it's also about building relationships with your audience. Here's how you can engage effectively:

Respond Promptly: Monitor comments, messages, and mentions on social media and respond promptly. Address inquiries, thank customers for their feedback, and provide helpful information.

User-Generated Content: Encourage customers to share their experiences with your products by reposting their content. User-generated content adds authenticity and social proof to your brand.

Behind-the-Scenes Content: Give your audience a glimpse behind the scenes of your business. Share stories about product creation, team members, and company values. Transparency fosters trust.

Measuring Success and Iterating

To ensure the effectiveness of your social media efforts, it's crucial to measure key metrics and iterate on your strategies. Here's how:

Analytics Tools: Use social media analytics tools to track metrics such as engagement rate, reach, clicks, and conversions. Analyzing these data points provides insights into what's working and what can be improved.

A/B Testing: Experiment with different types of content, posting times, and messaging to see what resonates best with your audience. A/B testing helps you refine your approach for better results.

Feedback and Adaptation: Listen to feedback from your audience and adjust your social media strategy accordingly. Stay agile and adaptive to changing trends and preferences.

Putting It into Action

Create a social media Calendar: Plan out your social media posts in advance, including product highlights, promotions, and interactive content. A calendar helps maintain consistency and organization.

Engage Authentically: When interacting with your audience, be genuine and authentic. Show appreciation for their support, address concerns transparently, and foster a sense of community.

Run Social Media Campaigns: Launch targeted campaigns to promote specific products or offers. Use eye-catching visuals, compelling copy, and clear calls to action to drive engagement and conversions.

Monitor and Analyze: Regularly review your social media analytics to track progress toward your goals. Identify trends, successes, and areas for improvement.

By harnessing the power of social media, you can amplify your presence on Facebook Marketplace, drive traffic to your listings, and cultivate a loyal customer base. Social media is not just a marketing tool; it's a platform for building relationships and creating a community around your brand. In the next chapter, we'll explore the importance of customer feedback and strategies for gathering valuable insights to improve your business on Facebook Marketplace.

Chapter Eleven

The Power of Customer Feedback and Insights

Customer feedback is a goldmine of valuable insights that can propel your business forward on Facebook Marketplace. In this chapter, we'll explore the importance of gathering feedback, strategies for collecting it, and how to leverage these insights to enhance your products, services, and overall customer experience.

Why Customer Feedback Matters

Customer feedback is a direct line to understanding your audience's needs, preferences, and pain points. Here's why it's crucial:

Insight into Customer Satisfaction: Feedback allows you to gauge how satisfied your customers are with their purchases and interactions with your brand.

Identification of Improvement Areas: It highlights areas of improvement, whether it's product quality, shipping times, customer service, or website usability.

Validation of Successes: Positive feedback reinforces what you're doing right and can serve as testimonials to attract new customers.

Strategies for Collecting Customer Feedback

There are various methods for gathering customer feedback, each offering unique insights. Here are some effective strategies to consider:

Surveys and Polls: Create online surveys or polls to gather structured feedback. Ask specific questions about product satisfaction, delivery experience, or suggestions for improvement.

Product Reviews and Ratings: Encourage customers to leave reviews and ratings on your Facebook Marketplace listings. Positive reviews boost credibility, while constructive feedback helps you improve.

Social Media Listening: Monitor social media mentions, comments, and messages related to your brand. This provides real-time feedback on customer sentiments and experiences.

Email Follow-Ups: Send follow-up emails after a purchase to gather feedback. Include a brief survey or simply ask for thoughts and suggestions. Personalize these emails for a higher response rate.

In-Person Events: If feasible, host in-person events or pop-up shops where customers can interact with your products. Use this opportunity to gather feedback directly.

Leveraging Customer Insights

Once you've collected feedback, it's essential to act on it strategically. Here's how you can leverage customer insights to improve your business:

Product Development: Use feedback to guide product improvements or new product development. Identify common pain points or desired features to enhance your offerings.

Customer Service Enhancements: Address any recurring issues raised in feedback to improve your customer service processes. This could involve additional training for staff or streamlining communication channels.

Optimizing Marketing Strategies: Insights from customer feedback can inform your marketing strategies. Tailor your messaging and promotions based on what resonates most with your audience.

Enhancing User Experience: Feedback on website usability or the shopping experience can guide website optimizations. Make it easier for customers to find what they're looking for and complete purchases.

Responding to Feedback

Effective feedback loops involve not just collecting feedback but also responding to it. Here's how to approach responding to customer feedback:

Timely Responses: Acknowledge and respond to feedback promptly, whether it's positive or negative. This shows that you value customer input.

Transparency and Empathy: Be transparent in your responses and show empathy towards customer concerns. Even if the feedback is negative, a thoughtful response can turn the situation around.

Implementing Changes: When appropriate, communicate changes or improvements based on customer feedback. This shows that you listen and take action to address their needs.

Creating a Feedback-Focused Culture

To truly benefit from customer feedback, it's essential to foster a culture within your business that values and prioritizes customer input. Here's how you can create a feedback-focused culture:

Training and Education: Educate your team on the importance of customer feedback and how to collect it effectively. Provide training on active listening and empathy in customer interactions.

Recognition and Rewards: Recognize and reward employees who excel in gathering and acting upon customer feedback. This encourages a proactive approach to customer satisfaction.

Feedback Loops: Establish structured feedback loops within your business. Regularly review customer feedback, share insights with relevant teams, and track progress on implementing changes.

Putting It into Action

Design Feedback Surveys: Develop customer feedback surveys tailored to different touchpoints, such as post-purchase, customer service interactions, or website usability.

Promote Reviews and Ratings: Encourage customers to leave reviews and ratings on your Facebook Marketplace listings. Offer incentives such as discounts for verified reviews.

Monitor Social Media Mentions: Use social media listening tools to monitor brand mentions and conversations.

Address any customer concerns or questions in a timely manner.

Implement Changes: Based on feedback insights, prioritize and implement changes to improve your products, services, or processes. Communicate these changes to your audience.

Celebrate Successes: Share positive feedback and success stories with your team. Celebrate improvements and milestones achieved through customer feedback.

By actively collecting and leveraging customer feedback, you can gain invaluable insights that drive business growth and customer satisfaction. Remember, listening to your customers is not just about hearing their voices; it's about using those voices to shape a better future for your business on Facebook Marketplace.

Chapter Twelve

A Roadmap to Continued Success on Facebook Marketplace

Congratulations on embarking on your journey to sell like crazy on Facebook Marketplace! As we conclude this book, let's recap the key takeaways from each chapter and provide you with a roadmap for continued success in your Marketplace endeavors.

Chapter 1: Understanding Facebook Marketplace

Introduced you to the basics of Facebook Marketplace and its benefits.

Provided an overview of Marketplace features and how to navigate the platform effectively.

Chapter 2: Creating an Uncontested Marketplace

Discussed identifying niche markets and conducting market research.

Explored strategies for positioning your products for success and setting yourself apart from competitors.

Chapter 3: Strategic Lead Generation

Highlighted the importance of targeted advertising and crafting compelling product listings.

Provided engagement tactics and tips for using Facebook Insights to generate leads.

Chapter 4: Building a New Customer Base

Covered converting leads into loyal customers and effective communication strategies.

Explored providing top-notch customer service and post-purchase engagement techniques.

Chapter 5: Establishing Product Dominance

Discussed building brand authority, fostering trust with buyers, and encouraging repeat purchases.

Explored leveraging reviews, testimonials, and strategies for scaling your business.

Chapter 6: Maximizing Sales with Advanced Techniques

Introduced cross-promotion strategies, running limited-time offers, and leveraging Facebook Groups.

Explored collaborations, partnerships, and advanced tips for increasing sales.

Chapter 7: Overcoming Challenges and Pitfalls

Addressed dealing with competition, handling customer disputes, managing inventory, and avoiding scams.

Covered staying compliant with Facebook policies to ensure a smooth selling experience.

Chapter 8: Future Trends and Innovations

Explored the evolving landscape of Facebook Marketplace and predictions for future trends.

Provided strategies for preparing your business for future success and innovations in e-commerce.

Chapter 9: Harnessing the Power of social media for Marketplace Success

Discussed building a strong brand presence on social media.

Explored leveraging social media marketing strategies, engaging with your audience, and measuring success.

Chapter 10: The Power of Customer Feedback and Insights

Emphasized the importance of gathering customer feedback and its role in improving your business.

Provided strategies for collecting feedback, leveraging insights, and creating a feedback-focused culture.

Chapter 11: Conclusion and Roadmap to Continued Success

As you continue on your journey to sell like crazy on Facebook Marketplace, here's a roadmap to guide you:

Stay Updated: Keep abreast of new features and updates on Facebook Marketplace. The platform is constantly evolving, and staying informed will give you a competitive edge.

Adapt and Innovate: Be ready to adapt your strategies based on trends and customer feedback. Innovation is key to staying ahead in the marketplace.

Engage with Your Audience: Continue to engage with your audience on social media and Facebook Marketplace. Building relationships and fostering a sense of community can lead to long-term success.

Monitor Performance: Regularly review your metrics and analytics to track your progress. Identify what's working well and areas for improvement.

Customer-Centric Approach: Always prioritize the needs and satisfaction of your customers. Their feedback and insights are invaluable for shaping your business strategies.

Continual Learning: Stay curious and open to learning new strategies and techniques. Attend webinars, workshops, and conferences to expand your knowledge.

Remember, success on Facebook Marketplace is not just about making sales; it's about building a thriving business that delivers value to your customers. By following the strategies and tips outlined in this book, you are well-equipped to achieve your goals and sell like crazy on Facebook Marketplace. Here's to your continued success!

Appendix

Resources and Tools

In this appendix, you will find a curated list of recommended tools, apps, useful links, websites, and a glossary of terms to support your journey as a successful seller on Facebook Marketplace.

Recommended Tools and Apps for Facebook Marketplace Sellers:

Canva: A user-friendly graphic design tool for creating eye-catching product images, banners, and promotional materials.

Hootsuite: A social media management platform that allows you to schedule posts, track engagement, and manage multiple social media accounts in one place.

Google Analytics: Track and analyze your website's traffic, customer behavior, and conversion rates to optimize your online presence.

Inventory Lab: Ideal for sellers managing inventory, this tool provides insights into profitability, sales trends, and inventory management.

Ship Station: Streamline your shipping process by integrating orders, printing labels, and managing shipments across multiple carriers.

Facebook Business Suite: A centralized dashboard for managing your Facebook and Instagram business profiles, including posting, messaging, and insights.

Later: Schedule and plan your Instagram posts in advance, ensuring a consistent and engaging presence on the platform.

Mailchimp: An email marketing platform to create newsletters, automated campaigns, and personalized messages to nurture customer relationships.

Sell Brite: Multichannel inventory management software that integrates with Facebook Marketplace.

Useful Links and Websites

Facebook Marketplace Seller Help Center: https://www.facebook.com/help/marketplace

Official resources and guidelines for Facebook Marketplace sellers.

Facebook Business Resources:
https://www.facebook.com/business/resources

Tools, insights, and success stories for businesses on Facebook.

Etsy Seller Handbook:

https://www.etsy.com/seller-handbook

Useful tips and guides for product photography, branding, and selling online.

Shopify Blog: https://www.shopify.com/blog

Articles on e-commerce trends, marketing strategies, and business growth.

eMarketer: https://www.emarketer.com –

Research and insights on digital marketing and e-commerce trends.

Moz: https://moz.com –

SEO resources and tools to improve your online visibility.

Small Business Administration (SBA): https://www.sba.gov

Resources for small business owners, including guides on business planning and funding.

Glossary of Terms

Lead Generation: The process of attracting and converting potential customers into leads.

Niche Market: A specific segment of the market with unique needs and preferences.

Cross-Promotion: A marketing strategy where two or more businesses promote each other's products or services.

A/B Testing: A method of comparing two versions of a webpage or marketing campaign to determine which performs better.

ROI (Return on Investment): A measure of the profitability of an investment, calculated as a ratio of net profit to the initial investment.

Conversion Rate: The percentage of website visitors who complete a desired action, such as making a purchase.

SEO (Search Engine Optimization): The process of optimizing a website to improve its visibility on search engines like Google.

User-Generated Content: Content created by users, such as reviews, testimonials, or social media posts.

Augmented Reality (AR): Technology that overlays digital information onto the real world, often used for virtual try-on experiences.

Influencer Marketing: Collaborating with social media influencers to promote products or services.

Cryptocurrency: Digital currency secured by cryptography, such as Bitcoin or Ethereum.

Customer Lifetime Value (CLV): The predicted total revenue a customer will generate over the entire relationship with your business.

Drop shipping: A retail fulfillment method where a store doesn't keep the products it sells in stock; instead, it purchases the products from a third party and ships them directly to the customer.

This appendix provides a handy reference for tools and resources that can aid in your Facebook Marketplace selling journey. Whether you're looking for apps to streamline your operations, useful websites for insights, or a glossary of terms to clarify industry jargon, this appendix has you covered.

Happy

selling!

www.ingramcontent.com/pod-product-compliance
Lightning Source LLC
Chambersburg PA
CBHW071050290526
45795CB00004B/1420

Chapter 2

Success Mindset Shift

"Failure is not something to be ashamed of, it's something to be powered by. Failure is the highest-octane fuel your life can run on." Even a brilliant executive at some stage has ever felt stuck in a rut, unable to move forward with your goals? Chances are, he or she needs a mindset shift. A mindset is a way of thinking that influences your behavior and view on life. For example, someone with a victim mindset might think, "The world is against me, bad things always happen to me," while someone with a hero mindset might think, "I can rise above my challenges."

It was Heraclitus the ancient Greek philosopher who hit the nail on the head when he said 'Change is the only constant in life'. As with most people who are still being quoted tens, hundreds & in this case thousands of years after they lived, the simplest of statements are often the most poignant, memorable, and impactful.

Success starts in the mind. Dreaming big is great, but without the right mindset, it's so much harder to reach your goals. A fixed mindset is the belief that your abilities and talents are set in stone and cannot be improved. A growth mindset, on the other hand, is the belief that you can develop your skills and abilities through effort and practice. A mindset shift involves reframing the way we think about our lives and our goals. It is an important tool for personal growth and development as it helps us to identify areas of our lives that need improvement and changes that will lead us to success.

Success is not linear. In life, there isn't an end goal. It's not a video game where we can reach the top level. We don't suddenly reach the finish line where we are crowned as "winners". There is no pot of gold waiting at the end of the rainbow. It's not a movie where we're working towards our happy ending. Along whichever route you take, there are always going to be bumps along the way. On that journey, the terrain is going to look very different each day, week, month, and year. It may feel like your levels of "success" in life fall for a while. But that doesn't mean they won't rise again. Success isn't going to be linear. For most of us, it's more of a rollercoaster ride. But we need to learn to ride out those troughs as well as the peaks.

Failure is an important part of success. No one enjoys failure. It can shake our confidence and hurt our self-esteem. But it can also toughen us up and help us learn important lessons. There's no getting around the inconvenient fact that success and failure are often inseparable. It's the failures along the way that allow us to tweak and correct our course, which leads us to greater success. Every screw-up teaches us what we don't want so that we can get a better understanding of what we do want.

It's never too late. A lot of people give up on their desires for life because they tell themselves they're to:

Old
Settled
Out of shape

Out of luck
Stuck in their ways

But in the words of George Eliot: "It's never too late to be what you might have been". The reality is that whilst there is still breath in your body then you always have the potential to learn, grow and expand. Having a growth mindset compared to a fixed mindset is like rocket fuel for success. The difference between the two ultimately comes down to your belief system. cause they've created a mind-made expiry date for success. The difference between the two ultimately comes down to your belief system.

A key part of having a successful mindset shift is recognizing self-imitation where your limitations lie. By being aware of these limitations, you can make more informed decisions on how best to overcome them. When we can identify the things that are holding us back, it becomes easier to take steps toward overcoming those obstacles and achieving our goals. This could involve taking classes or workshops, getting support from friends and family, or simply changing the way we think about ourselves and our situations.

When we experience a mindset shift, it often leads us to re-evaluate our goals or create new ones altogether. We may realize that what we originally set out to do isn't necessarily what is best for us in the long run. This realization can be empowering because it allows us to adjust our plans based on what works best for us rather than trying to conform to someone else's idea of success. We can also use this time of evaluation to focus on more realistic goals that will help us move forward in life in a positive direction.

Mindset shifts can also be used as an opportunity to change habits or routines that no longer serve us well. It's easy to get stuck in old patterns of behavior but by recognizing when something isn't working anymore, we have the chance to make changes and develop healthier habits that will benefit us in the future. For example, if you find yourself struggling with procrastination, shifting your mindset could be the first step towards forming better productivity habits such as making daily lists or setting strict deadlines for yourself!

When it comes to success in anything, you need a mindset that puts you in the right place at the right time. You can learn to apply the same principles by making small shifts in your thinking. But there are many pitfalls on the path to change. And a lot of them are rooted in your mindset. Our minds can be a tricky business–they can help us achieve feats we never thought possible, or they can hold us back from accomplishing what we know we can achieve.

Most Needed Mindset Shifts

Things don't always go as planned, but whether you bounce back and try again is up to you. If you're constantly feeling like you're a failure, then it's time for a mindset shift toward success.

Time Is Precious. There is never enough time in a day. There are a lot of things to do, and you want/need to be doing them all. You need to stop doing everything and focus on the right things. When we're getting busy, we're usually just moving from one urgent task to another. All tasks do not have a deadline when it comes to your long-term goals.

Choose to see the positive. The way we frame our day can either set us up for success or failure–and the thing is we have a choice. When you choose to focus on the good, you are creating a good day for yourself. Focusing on the positive doesn't mean ignoring the bad. When bad things happen, we can't ignore them. But we can acknowledge them, and not let those things ruin the rest of our day. So, if a co-worker sends a nasty email first thing in the morning, you can acknowledge that it made you feel pretty crappy. Then you can take a deep breath, find something to be grateful for, and move forward with your day without dwelling on that one thing and letting it ruin the rest of your day. And obviously, sometimes big things happen–we lose loved ones, get into car accidents–and these things are major. We can't just sweep them under the rug and put a smile on our faces. We have to sit with the hurt and the negative feelings. But when we have cultivated a habit of being positive when these catastrophic things happen, we can cultivate feelings of gratitude even while feeling hurt, sad, and upset. We might feel grateful for the bystander who stopped to help us after our car accident. Or the old family friend who brought food over after a loss. And these moments of gratitude can help anchor us amid emotional turmoil. So, start cultivating that positivity today.

Notice your self-sabotages. Have you ever noticed that when things are going great and everything is lining up, you get sick? Or did something break down? Do you ever feel like you are just waiting for the other shoe to drop? We all have blocks, and upper limits–the limits of what we think we can achieve/ deserve/ are worthy of. And when we get too close to those limits or reach them, we self-sabotage and prevent ourselves from really achieving those successes. Do you procrastinate planning your vacation and then when you do, airline tickets are way too expensive? Self-sabotage.

Do self-introspection. Most of the time, we set goals about things we want to accomplish—milestones, accolades, promotions, etc. But we don't think about what's behind those desires. And usually, those are feelings we want to experience or cultivate. The idea is that behind every desire is a feeling we want to have. Do you want that promotion at work? Maybe you want to be recognized, feel accomplished, or be successful. You don't have to have clear answers about how to get those feelings, but simply getting clear about how you want to feel can open you up to new possibilities.

Do it for the right reasons. The right reasons are essentially your reasons. It might sound obvious but success isn't success if it's someone else's version of it. Yet the truth is that so many of us end up chasing other people's dreams and not our own. Whether it's your parents, your peers, or simply society itself. We're told what makes us happy from such a young age:

Getting that promotion
Winning awards
Earning lots of money
Being seen as "somebody"

We are so often sold what success should look like, that we don't stop to think about our unique recipe for it and whether it will fulfill us. Achieving success will bring nothing to your life unless it's focused on what matters most to you. That means using plenty of self-awareness to get better acquainted with your core values. They

18

can be your guiding compass for figuring out what you want out of life.

Don't wait until you feel ready. Fear has a habit of trying to buy us more time. We tell ourselves that we will make a start "when". Often, it's when we have more time, when we know more, when we've learned more, when we have more money, etc. But the chances are, you will never feel ready. You don't need to know every step you will take along the way. You just need to know your next step. Start from there, and take some all-important action.

Stop talking and start acting. Many people talk about a good game. But that's where it ends. But as we all know; actions speak louder than words. Those actions certainly don't have to be huge. Pick out three small steps that you can take this week which will bring you closer to success. Then do them. And when you do, know that they don't have to be perfect. Not everything will work out the way you thought or hoped — and that's no big deal. It's ok to change your mind or start again A plan is something to work towards, but it's flexible rather than set in stone. When you see your ideas and actions as an experiment, an opportunity, or an adventure, it allows you to approach them with curiosity rather than expectation. Indeed, success often requires determination, but that doesn't have to be single-minded. It's equally important to adapt to stay resilient. That means you can always change your mind and start again. There isn't just one shot at happiness or success. There are infinite routes.

Belief is powerful. The false beliefs we hold are silently pulling our strings behind the scenes. They've been in the making most of our lives and we probably don't even think about:

Where do they come from
Whether they're even true

But they still hold us back regardless. They tell us stories about ourselves and the world that feel very real (whether they are or not). Unfortunately, they may tell us very unhelpful lies too. Your brain decides that it won't work, without even trying. It's even thought that as much as 97% of reported pharmaceutical side effects are down to so-called "nocebo" effects. The brain is expecting the worst — so that's what it gets. Getting to grips with your beliefs and choosing the ones that serve you can make a fundamental difference in your life. As can the next mindset hack on our list...

Don't forget what you already have. Expansion and growth are wonderful. But we shouldn't neglect what we already have. Because the truth is that nothing is ever enough if you cannot recognize what is right in front of you. Gratitude helps us to get into the frame of mind of abundance rather than scarcity. Far from being just a cheesy sentiment, there is stacks of scientific evidence that highlight the practical benefits of embracing more gratitude. We're talking about things like:

Improved sleep
Better moods and feeling happier
Reduced risk of disease and stronger immunity
Better at handling adversity

Stronger relationships

And there's no denying that these are all things that contribute to our successes in life.

Remember that you miss all the shots you don't take. Some of us are naturally better at taking risks than others. And that's fine if you're content with that. As we said in the beginning, everyone's idea of a successful life is different. But if you feel stuck, want something different, or are craving more, then learning to get out of your comfort zone is essential.

Steps in changing your mindset:

Acknowledge your limitations: The first step in changing your mindset is to acknowledge any limitations or beliefs you may have about yourself that are holding you back.

Set realistic goals: Setting realistic goals is key to achieving success. Make sure your goals are achievable and measurable, so you can track your progress and stay motivated.

Visualize your success: Visualization is a powerful tool for creating the life you want. Spend time each day visualizing yourself achieving your goals and living the life of your dreams.

Celebrate your successes: Celebrating your successes, no matter how small will help you stay motivated and keep striving for bigger and better things.

Surround yourself with positive people: The people you surround yourself with can have a huge impact on your mental health. Fill your circle with people who support and encourage you to reach your goals.

Practice self-care: Taking care of yourself is essential for maintaining a positive mindset. Make sure you're taking time to relax, practicing mindfulness, eating well, and getting enough sleep.

Identify your limiting beliefs: The first step to changing your mindset from fixed to growth is to identify any limiting beliefs you may have about yourself. These could be beliefs about your intelligence, capabilities, or potential for success.

Challenge your limiting beliefs: Once you've identified your limiting beliefs, it's time to challenge them. Ask yourself if these beliefs are true or if they're just holding you back from reaching your full potential.

Reframe your thoughts: Instead of focusing on what you can't do or what you don't know, reframe your thoughts to focus on what you can do and what you can learn with effort and practice.

Take action: Taking action is the only way to progress toward your goals. Break down big tasks into smaller milestones and start moving forward.

Learn from your mistakes: Mistakes are inevitable, but instead of beating yourself up, reflect on what you could've done differently and use it as an opportunity to grow.

Communicate. One of the most important strategies for avoiding complex failures is emphasizing a preference for speaking up openly and quickly in your family, team, or organization. Simply, make it psychologically safe to be honest about a small thing before it snowballs into a larger failure. Many organization's failures could have been prevented if people felt able to speak up earlier with their tentative concerns.

Chapter 3

Learn from Mistakes

Albert Einstein once said, "*Anyone who has never made a mistake has never tried anything new.*" "*We get more and more resilient each time we try something new, regardless of whether it works out,*" says McNally. "*We're expanding our capacity to tolerate discomfort, which causes our comfort zone to get bigger.*"

When we don't learn from our mistakes, we inflict unnecessary stress on ourselves and others, and we risk losing people's confidence and trust in us. Did Jordan only have this attitude towards basketball? Not at all. He applied the same attitude to failure to his business ventures and hobbies. His Nike Jordan-branded shoes, endorsements, restaurants, and car dealerships have made him a billionaire, but he has also failed numerous times throughout his business career — most notably as owner of the Charlotte Bobcats basketball team. Michael Jordan was arguably the greatest basketball player of all time. However, many aren't aware of the failures he experienced on his path to success — including being cut from his high-school Varsity team on account of his height! Jordan himself was famous for saying: "I've missed more than 9000 shots in my career. I've lost almost 300 games. 26 times, I've been trusted to take the game-winning shot and missed. I've failed over and over and over again in my life. And that is why I succeed." It's possible that we won't be the Michael Jordan in our respective fields and professions. But Jordan's mindset towards failure is reproducible, provided that we don't allow our ego to stand in the way of learning, we manage our emotions in response to failure and we keep striving to learn and grow from our mistakes — and even enjoy them!

No one is immune to making mistakes – we are human, after all! But if we simply apologize and carry on as before, we're in danger of repeating the same errors. Having tried and failed means we dared to try something new, since there are few, if any, new endeavors that guarantee success. "Making a mistake" is not the same thing as "failing." A failure is the result of a wrong action, whereas a mistake usually is the wrong action. So, when you make a mistake, you can learn from it and fix it, whereas you can only learn from a failure. Think back to the last mistake that you made at work. Even if it was a minor one, like spilling coffee on a document seconds before you were due to present it, you'll likely have felt a rush of panic and then had the inconvenience of putting things right.

Mistakes are a catalyst for innovation. If we need motivation to keep going after setbacks, we simply have to think of all the well-known people and the setbacks that they endured before finally reaching their goals. Research has found that organizations that encourage and reward new ideas, innovation, and risk-taking, attract those who are willing to go beyond what they already know and do, perform better. Workers at stagnant organizations that are tied to the status quo, often grow to feel frustrated, causing many to conclude that they are in the wrong environment.

By examining what didn't work, we can expand our imaginations and thinking processes. The best way to learn is by doing and the more things we attempt to do, the more we set ourselves up for learning. Psychologist, author, and educator, Martin Seligman, one of the proponents of the positive psychology movement did some ground-breaking work on optimism. He discovered that optimists view setbacks differently from pessimists. Optimists see setbacks as temporary, and don't take them personally. They don't see them as an indication there is something wrong with them. Viewing failures in this manner can help build our optimism.

One of the most important things people in recovery can remind themselves of is that their past does not define their future. Individuals must realize that they are not their mistakes or faults; they are not their addiction. Instead, recovery provides the opportunity to move forward. Post-treatment, individuals get a second chance to choose who they are and what they want to do with their life. Just because they experienced addiction does not mean they are doomed. Many people in recovery move forward and achieve their wildest dreams, despite what they have been through.

Develop realistic thoughts about mistakes. Seeing faults and mistakes resulting from something specific and external, rather than something internal, can help individuals look at their mistakes with a more positive and realistic frame of mind. When one makes a mistake and automatically equates it to failure, they are not helping themselves in the long run. The best thing to do to move forward is to reframe these thoughts of failure. Reminding oneself of the following can help one develop realistic thoughts about mistakes: "Mistakes are a sign that I am challenging myself to do something difficult." "I can handle my faults." "I can learn from my mistakes."

It's normal to feel frustration when experiencing faults and mistakes. However, for some people, this shame and frustration begin to run their lives, especially in recovery. When experiencing active addiction, many people do things they are not proud of, and when they stop using substances, this guilt and shame can be overpowering. Luckily, in recovery, individuals get the chance to reframe their faults and mistakes with a positive mindset. Even though their actions had negative outcomes, they can also find positivity and move forward. Some techniques can help individuals look at their faults and mistakes with a different outlook.

It is a paradox, some remain hard-pressed to find anyone who has made major contributions to our world, and who got it right the first time, instead, of finding a trail of setbacks, missteps, dead ends, and detours that finally lead them to the achievements that are so visible. The best way for an individual to reframe their faults and mistakes is to learn from them. But how does one do that? Here are the tips to do that:

1. Own Up to Mistakes

One cannot learn from their mistakes until one admits they have made one. While it can be hard to admit to the things done in active addiction, it is a necessary part of the process. Individuals need to recognize that their morals, values, and beliefs were not what they were struggling with addiction. The things done in the past do not reflect one's current self. An individual needs to recognize that they are now in recovery and making an effort to change.

2. Reframe the Error

How an individual views their mistakes can determine how they react to them and what to do next. It can be easy for one to view their faults in a negative light. However, reframing these mistakes as an opportunity to learn can motivate individuals to become more motivated and resilient in their recovery journey.

3. Analyze the Mistake

To learn from mistakes, individuals must analyze them honestly and objectively. It may help for an individual to ask themselves the following questions:

What were they trying to do?

What went wrong?

When did it go wrong?

Why did it go wrong?

4. Put Lessons Learned Into Practice

Learning from one's mistakes is one thing but putting them into practice is another. At this point of learning to reframe faults and mistakes, individuals may run into challenges. As humans, we are habitual creatures, and it can be easy to fall back into old routines.

Acting on what one has learned will require the discipline and motivation to change their habits. Doing so will help individuals avoid self-sabotage in the future and allow them to reap the rewards and benefits of the recovery process.

Putting lessons learned into practice means an individual will need to identify the skills, knowledge, resources, and tools that will keep them from repeating their mistakes.

Faults and mistakes can turn into all-consuming guilt if not moved through. No matter where you have been or what you have done, you can learn to reframe your faults and mistakes. Remembering that you are on a journey of change, and you can learn from any mistake you have made can help you move forward in your recovery journey.

Chapter 4 [one reading]
Strategies for Learning from Failure

"Countless works are trying to understand how people and products succeed," but, there is very little understanding of the role of failure." -

Albert-László Barabási

"I cannot fix on the hour, or the spot, or the look or the words, which laid the foundation. It is too long ago. I was in the middle before I knew that I had begun."

- Jane Austen, Pride and Prejudice

"Never give in, never give in, never, never, never, never give in. Nothing, great or small, large or petty, never give in except to convictions of honor and good sense. Never yield to force; never yield to the overwhelming might of the enemy."

— Winston Churchill

Historically, many of us have only associated 'failure' with intense, negative emotions. However, we can dilute that intensity by attaching the 'failure' label to other experiences in which we didn't meet the successful outcome we desired (the definition of 'failure') but also didn't consider it to be important enough to be a failure. By diluting the intensity of emotion that we associate with failure, we take away much of the power it holds over us. This can result in a decreased intensity of our fear response to new goals or experiences that involve a risk of failing, and it becomes easier to proceed without our fear of failure threatening to sabotage us.

Considering every occasion or mistake that led to not achieving our desired outcome as a failure, and in doing so removing the power that the word 'failure' holds over us. This counter-intuitive approach is surprisingly powerful at 'tricking' our mind and reducing the intensity of emotion it associates with the word 'failure'.

Goals and dreams may evolve with time as we grow and develop, and it takes courage to deviate from our current path to begin a new one. Quitting something that doesn't resonate with you isn't failure. It's a sign of self-awareness and a willingness to take action towards a more fulfilling life. It's a step that is worthy of respect given that we take it fully knowing that there is inevitably going to be scrutiny and judgment from others that threatens our ego, self-confidence and credibility.

Why learning from failure is your key to success?

Failure leads to learning because we're able to identify where we went off track. From there, we can implement new ideas, new approaches, and new strategies. All of this results in increased innovation and creativity, which aids us in our learning journey.

"Every winner begins as a loser," says Wang, associate professor of management and organizations at Northwestern's Kellogg School of Management, who conceived and led a study with his team, to create a mathematical model that can reliably predict the success or failure of an undertaking, the researchers also analyzed 46 years' worth of venture capital startup investments. "For every principal investigator," explains Wang, "we know exactly when they failed, and we know how badly they failed because we know the scores of the proposal. And we also know when they eventually succeeded, after failing over and over, and got their first grant."

Failure and fault are virtually inseparable in most households, organizations, and cultures. Every child learns at some point that admitting failure means taking the blame. That is why so few organizations have shifted to a culture of psychological safety in which the rewards of learning from failure can be fully realized.

Many executives believe that all failure is bad and that learning from it is pretty straightforward. The experts of organizational behavior think both beliefs are misguided. In organizational life, some failures are inevitable and some are even good. Successful learning from failure is not simple. It requires context-specific strategies. But first leaders must understand how the blame game gets in the way and work to create an organizational culture in which employees feel safe admitting or reporting on failure.

Strong leadership can build a learning culture—one in which failures large and small are consistently reported and deeply analyzed, and opportunities to experiment are proactively sought. Executives commonly and understandably worry that taking a sympathetic stance toward failure will create an "anything goes" work environment. They should instead recognize that failure is inevitable in today's complex work organizations

The wisdom of learning from failure is incontrovertible. Managers in the vast majority of enterprises be it pharmaceutical, financial services, product design, telecommunications, and construction companies; hospitals; and NASA's space shuttle program, among others—genuinely wanted to help their organizations learn from failures to improve future performance. However, they are not able to make a headway to harvest it. The reason: Those managers were thinking about failure the wrong way. Most executives believe that failure is bad. They also believe that learning from it is pretty straightforward: Ask people to reflect on what they did wrong and exhort them to avoid similar mistakes in the future—or, better yet, assign a team to review and write a report on what happened and then distribute it throughout the organization. These widely held beliefs are misguided. First, failure is not always bad. In organizational life it is sometimes bad, sometimes inevitable, and sometimes even good. Second, learning from organizational failures is anything but straightforward.

Learn from Failure

Choose to learn from failure. Of course, you may need to give yourself a bit of breathing space to let your emotional reaction settle down before you can learn anything. But once you have some distance, really look at what happened and your part in it. What can you take accountability for? What step did you fail to take? What do you wish you had done differently? After you've assessed the situation, mop up the mess! Offer an apology to whoever needs it. Say you are sorry and be clear about what you are learning. This can be the toughest part of dealing productively with a failure, and it is certainly the most impactful. If you are leaning out over the tips of your skis and challenging yourself and your team in big, bold ways, you are bound to make mistakes. Innovation is messy. But if you can work through a failure and find your way to the other side, you will be so much better for it. The greatest leaders learn from failure and never forget the lesson. In this way, you only have to make each mistake one time. Isn't that amazing news?

Considering every failure as feedback or a learning experience — "failing forward". This is one of the most well-known methods of reframing failure. Instead of simply focusing on how we failed, we consider why we failed — and we draw valuable insights from this. Silicon Valley tech start-ups operate in an incredibly challenging business environment. However, despite the high likelihood of failure, they've embraced the fact that innovation and learning often come through failure! Their *'fail fast, fail often, fail forward'* mantra has its flaws, but at its core is a testament to their awareness that failure is a vital stepping stone on the path to success.

Failure is simply life's way of saying that the actions we took didn't yield the outcome we desired, that we should change our strategy if we want to achieve different results, and that there are many lessons we can take from our 'failure' to help us eventually form our winning strategy. Looking at failure as a learning experience is incredibly potent. As a junior tennis player, losing tennis matches was an incredibly disheartening form of failure for Mac. However, his coach frequently pointed out, "You don't learn when you win; you learn when you lose!"

Our failures are simply lessons. And success is our reward for learning that lesson and applying it effectively. Once we do this, we progress to the next failure lesson. I consider these to be good failures — failures that occur as we strive to achieve a goal that is meaningful to us and arise as a result of progress towards that goal.

British Olympic rower, Ben Hunt-Davis, in his book, '*Will It Make The Boat Go Faster?*' refers to our ability to '*bounce back*' from failures and setbacks. In the context of reframe, it doesn't matter how well you bounced back, but simply that you bounced back at all! This awareness helps us to recognize that we have the resilience to handle failure and the capability to bounce back from failure, increasing our confidence in our ability to repeat this if needed. Once we've developed this confidence, it becomes easier to look back and analyze our past failures using the feedback/learning experience reframe to glean how well we bounced back — and then learn the valuable lessons that will enable us to bounce back better from future failures.

Why could not learn from failure?

They jettisoning old cultural beliefs and stereotypical notions of success and embracing failure's lessons. Organizations need new and better ways to go beyond superficial lessons ("Procedures weren't followed") or self-serving ("The market just wasn't ready for our great new product").

Say No Blame Game

Leaders can begin by understanding how the blame game gets in the way. If people aren't blamed for failures, what will ensure that they try as hard as possible to do their best work? This concern is based on a false dichotomy. A work culture that makes it safe to admit and report on failure coexists with high standards for performance. In organizations, there exists a list of failures that range from deliberate deviation to thoughtful experimentation. Which of these causes involve blameworthy actions? Deliberate deviance, first on the list, obviously warrants blame. But inattention might not. If it results from a lack of effort, perhaps it's blameworthy. But if it results from fatigue near the end of an overly long shift.

Building a Learning Culture

Indeed, tolerance is essential for any organization that wishes to extract the knowledge such failures provide. But failure is still inherently emotionally charged; getting an organization to accept it takes leadership. Only leaders can create and reinforce a culture that counteracts the blame game and makes people feel both comfortable with and responsible for surfacing and learning from failures. They should insist that their organizations develop a clear understanding of what happened—not of "who did it"—when things go wrong.

Detecting & Analyzing Failure

Spotting big, painful, expensive failures is easy. Once a failure has been detected, it's essential to go beyond the obvious and superficial reasons for it to understand the root causes. This requires the discipline—better yet, the enthusiasm—to use sophisticated analysis. Leaders

36

must see that their organizations don't just move on after a failure but stop to dig in and discover the wisdom contained in it.

Promoting Experimentation

The third critical activity for effective learning is strategically producing failures—in the right places, at the right times—through systematic experimentation. Exceptional organizations are those that go beyond detecting and analyzing failures and try to generate intelligent ones for the express purpose of learning and innovating. It's not that managers in these organizations enjoy failure. But they recognize it as a necessary by-product of experimentation. They also realize that they don't have to do dramatic experiments with large budgets. Often a small pilot, a dry run of a new technique, or a simulation will suffice.

Failures trigger emotional distress, anxiety, and even depression. Yet, some people are more resilient than others. As they are less prone to perfectionism and less likely to hold themselves to unrealistic standards. If you expect to do everything perfectly or to win every contest, you will be disappointed or even distressed when it doesn't happen. In contrast, if you expect to try your best, accepting that you might not achieve everything you want, you're likely to have a more balanced and healthy relationship with failure.

Most of us do not know how to stop to challenge our spontaneous emotional responses to the events in our lives. It is learnable, and it's a crucial skill to bring more learning and joy into your life. Imagine you join a community tennis team—hoping to have fun and improve your skills. Arly on you'll make many mistakes and fail to return many of your opponents' shots. How should you feel? Despondent? Of course not. You force yourself to remember that you're simply trying to get better at a new activity.

Even when people work hard and are committed to doing the right thing, failure is always possible in a new situation. Sure, sometimes failures are caused by people who are careless or don't work hard, but even hard work can fail when a situation is new and different or some unexpected event happens. Sometimes sheer luck allows you to mail it in and succeed anyway. Our modern brains fail to distinguish between the fear of rejection which is irrational in most settings and more rational fears, such as that of an oncoming bus barrelling toward you on a city street.

The amygdala is a paired structure (the two are considered one brain area) inside your temporal lobe. It's a key part of emotional control and processes. It also plays a role in memory and learning. Fear activates the amygdala, as previously noted, inducing the fight-or-flight response, where "flight" does not necessarily mean running away but instead doing what you can to avoid looking bad.

Our brains fail to distinguish between the fear of rejection which is irrational in most settings and more rational fears, such as that of an oncoming bus barrelling toward you on a city street. This survival mechanism in our brains helped us elude saber-toothed tigers in prehistoric times, but today often leads us to overreact to harmless stimuli and to shy away from constructive risk-taking. Fear inhibits learning. It is hard for people to do their best work when they're afraid. It's especially hard to learn from failure because doing so is a cognitively demanding task.

Often, we think of failure as personal: "I am a failure." But when you feel like you are failing at work, it doesn't mean you are a failure. It's only natural to take it personally, though. For starters, your confidence can take a hit when you make a mistake. And failure causes stress. When you are stressed or reactive, you are prone to being problem-focused and may lose your ability to think well. You may also feel like a victim, which only further blocks your creativity. Your creativity and sensibility can help you to see fresh choices and paths forward — but not if it's blocked. Having skill amid failure can help you regain power and get your feet back under you. It can help you to work productively with a failure without thinking you are one.

We have to rewrite our understanding of success, showing the key role failure plays in it, and finally offering a methodological and conceptual framework to put failure where it belongs within the canon of success. The world gives a lot of opportunities for growth and personal development. We're on this collective journey to better ourselves and the world around us. But to do so, we need to fail. It's important to learn from failure because it brings us one step closer to reaching success. It's been cited that one in four entrepreneurs fail at their business before succeeding.

By definition, failure means that we didn't achieve success. It forces us back to square one, more often than not. But after failing, we know that we can't

39

approach the same task or goal in the same way. We wouldn't achieve the same result. So, the act of failure inevitably leads to thinking of new ways to overcome obstacles.

Failures often lead to success because they allow you to test and try what doesn't work to discover what does. Experiencing failure might be painful initially, though without it, you might miss the many benefits it can bring, including these ways that failures can lead to success:

Failure forces us to examine what went wrong. Reflection is an important part of failure. Without reflection, we wouldn't learn. It's important that after we fail, we take a moment to sit with it. What about the failure went well? What didn't go well? Where can we pinpoint what went wrong? It helps us to figure out how to course correct and do it better the next time.

Failure is getting space to innovate and redirect. As the phrase goes, we can't keep doing the same thing and expect the same results. Innovation is critical to learning. But to innovate, we need to know what went wrong. Failure often allows you to examine what worked or what didn't even more so than success. It can foster your critical and analytical thinking skills, allowing you to innovate, redirect, and try another way to execute something the next time. You might consider an option you otherwise wouldn't have if you succeeded on the first try. For example, many inventors and well-known businesspeople used failure as an inspiration to create something better than they originally intended, like modern technologies including iterations of the smartphone, early social media platforms, and virtual reality gaming systems.

Redirection also helps you discover more successful options. Think of navigating a maze blindfolded, for example. To find the exit, you likely take many wrong turns, though ultimately, they help you move through the maze and get to the exit. Similarly, in life, failing at something might redirect you to something greater.

Failure fosters Earning the opportunity to cultivate courage and resiliency. Those who experience hardship often develop more resiliency, determination, and courage than those who don't. Failure rarely means the end of something and usually, it's often the beginning. For example, you might interview for a promotion and be disappointed when you learn another colleague got the job instead. Using the experience to review your talents, skills, and abilities, you might focus on strengthening your professional capabilities and dare to apply for the next promotion. Alternatively, your employer might recognize how you handled the situation and create a role specifically with you in mind.

Having the option to try again. Failure can turn into success solely because of the option to try again repeatedly. Determination and focus often increase after experiencing setbacks, especially when you are close to attaining your ambition. You might accomplish your goal on the second attempt or it might take several tries. Even if it feels like it's not working, consider trusting in the process of turning failure into success. It's common to learn more each time you try something, so be willing to take another chance even after experiencing failure.

41

Gaining wisdom and room to learn and progress. You can often gain new insight, skills, and techniques through experiencing hardships or failures. For example, you might work on a technology project that malfunctions the first few days after launch, and your team conducts a thorough study of what went wrong and how to prevent it in the future. If you work on a project with setbacks again, you likely have the capabilities to fix or avoid the issue even more than a colleague whose projects were successful immediately.

Everyone fails in life. At one point or another, you may be going to suffer through failure. Most people associate failure with complete defeat. When we fail, we learn. We grow and mature, achieving new understandings and perspectives on life, love, business, money, relationships, and people. We're forced to make new connections, bridging gaps where we hadn't connected the dots before.

However, if you're going through failure right now, you might not find its utility at this moment. Wading through failure hurts. The pain can run so deep, that at times, you question your very existence. But there's most certainly light at the end of the tunnel. Still, lessons learned through failure are some of the most invaluable lessons you could garner in life.

When you fail, and you fail big, it feels like the end of the line. It feels like everything you once hoped for and dreamed of is now completely out of your reach. That takes an emotional toll on you. And it breaks you physically, mentally, and spiritually. And, while hindsight is 20/20, the perspective gained from failure is second to none. Most of the time, we're worried more about the fear of failure rather than the failure itself. What will others think?

Failure helps to redefine your priorities in life. Failure will either make you or it will break you. But it can't make you until it breaks you. That's the tricky part. No one has experienced a wild sense of success without first failing in a major way. While some have had to endure only a few failures before success, others have endured thousands. But when you fail, something strange happens. You begin to redefine your priorities in life, reordering the things that matter to you. You look inward, forcing an inventory of your hopes and your dreams. And you come to realize the things that matter the most to you. For most, this redefinition of priorities is a crucial step for overcoming failure. You shuffle things around to make room for what's important. If success is as important to you as you think, then you begin to make the necessary adjustments.

Failure shapes what you value. When you value the wrong things, success can be fleeting. It's easier to give up. But, when your values are in order, you can happily succeed rather than succeeding to be happy. Whenever we're focused on taking something from the world or other people, failure is only a moment away. But, when our values change to ones based on contribution, and giving more to the world than we receive, a monumental tectonic shift occurs.

Failure makes you more compassionate. We all know the power of the mighty ego. Before we fail in a major way, the ego runs your life. You're more concerned with what people think of you or how much money you spend in the face of others. But when you fail, things change. Major failure causes the ego to shatter. As a result, you become more compassionate. You become more in touch with your fellow human beings. It forces you to look deeper at things, understanding and caring more about others rather than solely focusing on yourself.

Failure improves your perspective on finance. Every major failure helps you look at money differently. Whether you fail at marriage, business, relationships, or anything else. You're forced to improve your perspective on all things money-related. All of the decisions we make in life have an impact on our bottom line. When we disrespect money and treat it with wonton disregard, it brings the potential for failure closer. When you add things like gambling, alcohol, and other addictions to the mix, it only amplifies your chances for failure.

By failure, you're forced to revise your approach. The goals shouldn't change, but your plan should be constantly evolving. Take an airplane for example. A plane takes off from LAX, flying to JFK. It plans to arrive 5.5 hours later by traveling at a particular speed, altitude, and direction. But what happens when there are interruptions along the way? Turbulence? Air-traffic congestion? The plane adjusts its plan. It doesn't change the goal.

When you fail, you develop new ways to cope with your emotions. The wild gyrations of success and failure can wreak havoc on your emotions. It's hard to stay focused and committed when you're upset and reeling from the pain of failure. Your emotions can be all over the place, up and down like a rollercoaster ride. But you find some important tools for coping with my emotions. You learn how to refocus and retrain your mind to see positive things rather than negative ones. The mind is very much like the lens of a camera – it will see whatever you focus on. When you train your mind to focus on the right things, you can better cope with the emotions that might make their way to the surface.

You re-envision your goals on failure. Don't think that your goals should be changed, even if you fail. It doesn't matter how lofty your goals might be. What I found through failure was that I had to re-envision my goals, not revise them. Value goal setting. Setting goals, the right way is a key factor in your potential for success. You need to go back and re-envision the goals. When you re-envision and take a step back, you gain more perspective. You see things clearer. Then, you can push forward full steam ahead. As long as you don't give up, you don't fail. It was just a temporary defeat. A setback, if you will.

Failure causes you to seek inspiration through others. Whether it's through famous people who failed at first or some other source, you begin to seek out things that will help push you toward your goals. If you've failed, you too should realize that many others have been through similar, if not worse, failures in the past. Seek and you shall find the inspiration that you're after. You may realize, through failure, that you weren't an effective manager at a given time. Possibly, it's through proper time management that you will be able to succeed. Considering that we all have an equal amount of time in the world, you know I have to make some changes, and fast.

Since no one person has more time than the other, it's the great equalizer in life. While everything else might be different, the amount of time we have is the same. Quickly realize that it was all about what you chose to do with that time that mattered, not how much you thought you had. You may practice a quadrant time management system to start by auditing your time for the first two weeks. And categorized everything you did, placing them into one of the four quadrants based on urgency and importance. Then, assess the results, and follow the system until it becomes a habit.

You figure out ways to better plan your day. Make to-do-list. First, read your long-term goals. Then ask yourself the following question, "What did I achieve today?". "Did I achieve my goals for the day?" Did I stick to my massive action plan? So, you learn to get organized, in more ways than one. It's the small things that count, which you do daily that lead to eventual success. This is also known as your most important task (MIT) of the day. When you tackle your MITs at the beginning of the day, you build momentum. You also feel more accomplished knowing that you got the big thing out of the way. If you have trouble with procrastination, then eat the frog! Your mind is clearest in the morning, so do it first thing.

You begin to look at obstacles differently. We're an instant gratification society. We want things and we want them now. We're somewhat similar to babies and toddlers in that respect. It's part of the psychology of our mind because we're born solely with the Id, which is the basal and instinctive part of the mind that acts on the pleasure principle. But that Mind is still very prevalent in us as adults. But, when you fail, you begin to realize that good things don't come overnight. We can't have our cake and eat it too. We have to work hard to accomplish our dreams and realize our goals.

When a person fails so many times over, he or she begins to realize this more and more. The problem? When goals are new, they're exciting. But when that newness wears off, the grind becomes far more real. We get bored, complacent, fed up, and we revert to our old ways. Our goals go out the window. But, when you can override that natural tendency, that's when the magic starts to happen. Not overnight, but in time.

You learn not to take 'no' for an answer. After a few major failures, you come to certain realizations about what people say they want and what they want. You learn not to take 'no' for an answer. You keep pushing and prodding, no matter what it takes. Often, you become so passionate that you can just about taste success. If you fail, it's not the end of the road. It's a new beginning. It's the chance to pick yourself back up again and try again, but this time with all the knowledge, wisdom, and experience you garnered from the last several tries.

You recognize your bad habits. When you fail, you destroy a part of your ego. Depending on how monumental that failure was, you lose either a major chunk or a small piece of your precious ego. Once that ego is shattered as a result of failure, you begin to recognize your bad habits. Bad habits get in the way of your failure. Bad habits can all but ruin our chances for success in anything. Part of your failures may be the results of bad habits that were ingrained in me for years and years. But you learn to recognize those bad habits. And when success means enough to you, you begin to change. You slowly modify your behavior over time to help rid yourself of any bad habit that is holding you back from success.

Remember that failing does not make us a failure. "I have failed", "I am failing", and "I might fail" are behavior statements. They're simply things that we tend to do, to the extent that they may have become habits.

Fragrant Palm Leaves: out of a fear of the unknown, we would rather identify with what is familiar, regardless of whether that identity is no longer serving us. However, our identities are much deeper-rooted. Not only are they harder to change; we don't necessarily want to change them because they make us who we are. To paraphrase a beautiful quote by Vietnamese Zen-Buddhist monk, Thich Nhat Hanh in his book, So, yes — you are permitted to fail. But you are not a failure.

Teaching others the lessons failure has taught us — creating purpose in failure. Many of us perceive failure to be without purpose, despite the lessons it can teach us. This is understandable. Life is short. We want to spend more time enjoying our success, not suffering because of our failures. After all, even if we succeed in the future as a result of the lessons we learned from failures, at this moment in time, we don't know if that success is guaranteed — let alone when! We hope it will happen, and that success will feel even more satisfying because of the rough road we've taken to reach it...but what can we do in the meantime to create purpose in our failures? One of the most powerful tools to create purpose in any experience is to use it to teach, inspire, and empower others to achieve their goals, overcome similar obstacles, and convey that they too can discover strength by confronting their failures, insecurities, and vulnerabilities.

Tips for turning failures into successes

1. Don't give up

We've all been there. A failure particularly stings and we want to just throw in the towel. Be persistent in pursuit of your dreams. It might take some reframing of perspectives. For example, can you break your big goal into little wins?   "If you recently failed at something, give yourself a moment to process it, feel the emotions whatever they may be, and then work to reframe the perceived failure as an opportunity for growth. Ask yourself, 'What did I learn from that?' It is ultimately about cultivating a growth mindset and celebrating the effort rather than the result."

You learn to never give up. Know the proverbial cliche, "Never give up." But, while it sounds mundane and over-repeated, it's entirely true. When you harbor deep enough meanings for succeeding, you learn to never give up, no matter what the situation. No matter how many times people laugh at you, walk all over you, or just plain ignore you, you just keep pushing. It doesn't matter if we only progress just a little bit each day. What matters is that we make some progress at all. We can't just stop.

2. Adopt a growth mindset

You have to want to learn to learn from failure. To do this well, you need to adopt a growth mindset. A growth mindset embraces challenges. It perseveres even in failures. People can learn, change, and adapt. It wants to learn and grow. It accepts and embraces constructive feedback and constructive criticism. And it's not easy. But a fixed mindset doesn't set up anyone for success. Think of ways you can change your perspective around your day-to-day interactions as a start.

3. Practice Inner Work

The science behind Inner Work shows incredible mental fitness benefits. Inner Work looks different for everyone. For example, a 30-minute walk in the morning can be your daily Inner Work. Or a week away from work while you take advantage of your unlimited PTO. Or just a three-minute journaling session or mindful moment. Embed Inner Work into your daily habits. You'll find better clarity, more productivity, increased creativity and innovation, and more.

4. Be courageous

During the most recent Winter Olympics, a video of a four-year-old going snowboarding went viral. The father of the little girl hooked her up to a microphone to record her positive self-talk while she cruises down the mountain. In the video, you can hear her say, "I won't fall. Maybe I will. That's OK 'cause we all fall."To fail takes courage. But to try again after failure takes even more. It's OK if you fail (and then fail again). But have the courage to get up and try and try again.

5. Build mental fitness

Hand-in-hand with a growth mindset comes mental fitness. Look at failure as a learning journey. What skills can you pick up along the way? What tools can you add to your toolbox? What new things can you take away from your failures? Start building your mental fitness plan with failures as part of your journey. With increased mental fitness, you'll find yourself better equipped to weather the ups and downs of life. Better Up can help you on your mental fitness journey.

Handling professional failure takes effort, acceptance, and action. Here are a few tips on how to turn failure into success:

Think of failure as a tool. Consider changing your mindset about failure and instead think of it as a tool to help you determine what works and what doesn't. Viewing it as an opportunity to innovate rather than as a determent to success can help you accept and use failure to your advantage.

Separate failing from failure. Many consider failing and failure as different concepts, with failing as the act of trying something you learn doesn't work and failure is the act of giving up and not continuing to try. Thinking of them as separate terms can help you stay motivated toward success.

Define what success means to you. Knowing what you want to achieve and how you measure success can also help you determine your outlook on what defines failure or how to move past it.

Keep it professional. Often how you handle a failure or error in a professional setting matters more than the mistake itself, so consider keeping a professional demeanor and exercise emotional intelligence. Remain composed, mindful, and understanding of the situation.

Take responsibility. Owning your failure often is a sign of maturity and professionalism, both of which are powerful qualities in achieving success.

Have confidence and stay committed. While others can help you achieve success and move past failure, most of the work and accomplishments come from within. Stay self-confident in your abilities and continue to work hard toward your professional goals, outlining the steps and actions it takes to achieve them.

Move forward rather than dwelling on it. Consider alternative options and take action to address the failure you experienced. Working to correct a mistake rather than dwelling can often help you get motivated and achieve success faster than continually thinking about what went wrong.

Take a break and then set new goals. It's okay to pause after experiencing failure, and it can help you gain perspective on what lessons there are to learn from the situation. Afterward, consider creating an action plan and setting specific goals, organizing yourself, and focusing on the next steps to take toward achieving your original desired outcome or a new victory.

Chapter 5

Strategies to Reframe Failure

Thomas Edison famously said, "I have not failed. I've just found 10,000 ways that won't work." At the time that he was struggling to invent the light bulb, Edison was derided and ridiculed by the media as a great failure. The quote above was Edison's response to a reporter asking him why he persisted and didn't give up. Edison had been able to reframe failure to his advantage. Rather than see it as a disadvantage, or obstacle, he was able to see the value in it.

Colonel Sanders, the founder of KFC was famously rejected 1,009 times before someone agreed to his franchise chicken model. But he knew, deep down inside, that his product was superior. He harbored the belief that eventually, people would start to say yes.

Henry Ford's first two companies failed. The first one went bankrupt. And the second one he had to walk away from with only the rights to his name after a big dispute. But it was his third try that sealed the deal. He was so passionate about his mission that he refused to give up.

It's a natural progression to become more passionate about your mission the more times you fail. It's a result of refining the ideas in your mind, solidifying them in thought, and making them far more real and concrete.

Framing is the way you perceive and present a situation, based on your beliefs, assumptions, emotions, and expectations. Reframing is the process of changing your frame, by adopting a different viewpoint, finding a new meaning, or discovering a positive aspect. For example, if you fail a test, you can frame it as a disaster that ruins your chances of success, or you can reframe it as feedback that shows you what you need to improve.

The way you frame and reframe your failures can have a significant impact on your motivation, self-esteem, resilience, and growth. If you frame your failures negatively, you may feel discouraged, ashamed, or hopeless, and avoid taking risks or trying new things. If you reframe your failures positively, you may feel encouraged, curious, or hopeful, and seek new opportunities or challenges. Reframing can also help you cope with stress, anxiety, and frustration, and foster a growth mindset that embraces learning from mistakes.

Reframing failure is a life-enhancing skill that helps us overcome our spontaneous aversion to failure. It begins with the willingness to look at yourself—not to engage in extensive self-criticism or to enumerate your flaws, but to become more aware of universal tendencies that stem from how we're wired and are compounded by how we're socialized. It needs to take a look at some of your idiosyncratic habits. Without this, it's hard to experiment with practices that help us think and act differently.

Acknowledge a failure, no matter its size. To work productively with a failure is to acknowledge that it has happened. Tell the truth — to yourself and others. As Chris Cardinal writes, "*We're conditioned to focus on "big" failures: a failed product launch, lost sale, or any other unmistakable instances of falling short.*

When a miss doesn't rise to that level of failure, we're often biased to consider it "close enough" or at least a draw. It's too easy to dismiss the small failures or missteps. If they don't carry a significant cost, or if they're fairly easily resolved, then we can brush them off as typical.

Naming something a failure and bringing a measure of objectivity to the telling of it takes a certain amount of grit and courage. And that's exactly what gets built each time you name it. Over time, you not only become more resilient in the face of setbacks, you help create a workplace culture that has a healthier relationship to failure. As a result, you get more and more comfortable naming it without spiraling into shame.

In his book "Teaching Smart People to Learn", Chris Argyris observes, "*Failure forces you to reflect on your assumptions and inferences. So, when smart people do fail — or merely underperform — they can be surprisingly defensive. Instead of critically examining their own behavior, they cast blame outward — on anyone or anything they can.*"

Sidestep the blame game, which is only likely to send you into a tailspin of anger and regret. Look past failure without trying to lay blame on anyone (including yourself). While you shouldn't be defensive, you also shouldn't blame yourself. Remember, you are not a failure. If you tell yourself that you are a failure, you're unlikely to engage the emotional distance necessary to objectively reflect on what happened and learn from it. A healthy way to reframe mistakes is to see the errors as experiences an individual can learn something from. One can ask themselves how this mistake can add to their life. How can this mistake shape their future decisions and help them grow? While it can be challenging, it is crucial not to let errors define individuals and their lives.

It's just as important to collapse what's happening or happened from your self-worth. Most successful people strived due to their failures, and without them, they wouldn't end up where they are today. By taking stock of our accomplishments, and our setbacks, we can better understand ourselves, our skills, and our growth ahead.

Reframing failure, especially at work, can be easier said than done. Look for the opportunity within failure. What does failure tell us about our work, ourselves, and those we are working with? If we are looking for opportunities to continuously learn, we will discover aspects of what doesn't work in all of our failures that will lead us closer to what will ultimately work. Instead of looking at setbacks strictly as failures, consider thinking of them as an experiment that gives us valuable information that we can draw upon to move forward. Edison did it.

"*Thinking of failure as part of the process normalizes the experience and makes it an expectation, rather than an exception,*" says Dr. Melanie McNally, a psychologist.

Chapter 6

How to Deal with Failure

"Only those who dare to fail greatly can ever achieve greatly."   —Robert F. Kennedy

There may be times when you experience failure in academics, job, workplace, or business. So, it's important to learn skills to cope with and overcome these challenges. It's important to deal with failure to prevent negative emotions such as anger, embarrassment, or anxiety from having a lasting effect on yourself and others. These emotions can affect relationships and decisions, making it a challenge to overcome failure and progress.

What is failure? A fairly common understanding of failure is setting a goal but not achieving it. We tend to believe that knowing whether or not you achieved a goal is fairly simple. It's often based on data. However; that common definition of being in failure mode as "not achieving a goal" isn't so accurate and straightforward, after all. Imagine yourself in each of the following three scenarios and whether you'd consider yourself to have failed:

First: An experienced marathon runner sets a goal to run her next marathon in under four-and-a-half hours. This goal is a full 15 minutes shorter than her prior best time. She completes the marathon in 4 hours and 36 minutes. Besting her prior record by nine minutes.

Second: A senior director seeks a promotion to VP and competes against other internal and external candidates. She receives positive feedback. However, she gets told that the leadership team felt that hiring an external person would demonstrate their commitment to change.

Third: A top young professional at an organization gets asked to prepare a slide deck for a high-profile meeting. He submits what he considers to be an excellent presentation to his boss. The boss praises the work but substantially changes the slides before the big meeting.

Notice that the differentiator in all three of these failure analysis examples is an ideal we've set in our minds. Measuring goal achievement can be a subjective and political activity. In each of these examples above, you can sense that the individuals tried hard and performed well in their efforts. Thus, the definition of being in failure mode as "not achieving a goal" isn't so accurate and straightforward, after all. But in truth, failure is often in the eye of the beholder. We all experience failure. But only some people know how to learn from it to be more successful in the future.

Failure is understood as a lack of success or the inability to meet an expectation. The expectation we fail to meet is often our own or one that we've created in our head. Most of us don't set out looking to fail at anything. And we especially don't want to be labeled as a failure. But maybe that is a mistake. Failure can be useful. We can learn from it, gain new insights, and do better next time. The right kind of failures give us new information and teach us something that gets us closer to our goals.

Life is a roller coaster- we all experience moments of success and happiness as well as occasions of failure and sadness. Furthermore, people often fear failure, and when this experience comes about, do not have the proper tools to cope and move forward. Nonetheless, we should change the perspective of failure, since without it we would be less capable of compassion, empathy, kindness, and high achievement.

Some live by the motto: If you aren't failing you aren't taking big enough risks. Said another way, if everything you try turns out exactly as planned and feels very comfortable, you probably aren't stretching yourself. And if you aren't stretching, you aren't growing.

The in-depth research studies suggest the following to overcome failure.

Accept feelings and emotions

Failure is linked with feelings and emotions such as sadness, anxiety, stress, rage, and so on. Those feelings are incredibly uncomfortable for any person and will do anything to get rid of them. However, the truth is that those feelings and emotions will help you work harder to find different and better solutions so you will improve next time. Go ahead and embrace those feelings and emotions, avoiding them can lead to unhealthy coping mechanisms!

Failure does not mean your life is going to be over

Many people believe that failure defines who you are and your future; that statement is not true at all! The truthfulness is that failure is what happens to you, not what is you. We all fail in life in different aspects of life, for instance, job experiences, love life, getting into a university, and other things. You do not need to let your failures define you, that is completely optional.

Learn from failure and be constructive

Learning from failure is one of the biggest challenges and lessons you will have in your life. Understanding what you did wrong will help you mentally more potent than ever and establish specific goals with astonishing strategies. You fail and learn. You fall and get up again. You recuperate, get ready to stand up, and achieve your goals.

Find inspiration

Get out of the place you are right now and forget your failure. Travel to a different part of the world and get to know multiple people. Most of the time, when individuals find inspiration, they forget about the past and become motivated in the future. If you find yourself inspired, no one, or anything, will stop you. It helps to get out of your mind and focus on outside sources of information which will give you a newfound perspective.

Don't give up

Make yourself comprehend giving up is never going to be an option. Make yourself happy and appreciate the time. Prove to yourself you are capable of doing anything you want and demonstrate with your actions that the nay-sayers are wrong. Most importantly, success comes to individuals who keep trying and don't give up.

Be passionate

An answer for failure, on some occasions, may have a connection with a lack of passion for something. Otherwise, if you are passionate about something, you will be motivated and put in a lot of effort. Be passionate about something you love and not because of what is imposed on you by others.

Surround yourself with positive people

Your environment can make a huge difference in how you confront and cope with failure. Surround yourself with people who motivate you continuously. Your mind is dealing with stress and anxiety, so the best way to not have another burden is to be accompanied by positive people.

Avoid isolating yourself

It is ubiquitous when people fail to be sad, depressed, upset, anxious, and stressed. Therefore, it is vital to be surrounded by people and feel free to express yourself. There are multiple ways to be surrounded by individuals such as family, friends, positive groups, and others. Do not forget that your mental health is crucial. When experiencing a failure, try to alter your perspective to not only avoid future missteps but also recognize that although failures happen, they don't define you. By taking time to acknowledge and accept failure, along with the varied emotions that may come with it, you can better process those feelings and overcome them.

Acknowledge your feelings

It's common to avoid the feelings associated with failure since they can cause discomfort, but it's important to learn how to acknowledge them instead. Allow yourself to recognize your feelings and name them. If it's disappointment or anger you feel, try to understand where the feeling stems from and what you can learn from it.

Example: Maria didn't get the promotion she had hoped for and she feels let down by her inability to stand out. Maria analyzes her feelings and learns that her disappointment isn't in herself but in her expectation of getting the job. She sets goals to improve her productivity to stand apart from her colleagues, rather than assuming she already did.

Recognize irrational beliefs

After experiencing a failure, you may have more negative thoughts, but it's important to note that these feelings and beliefs may not be rational. One way to combat these thoughts is to reflect on your successes. Compile a list of successes, no matter how small, and consult it before the next task or when you feel fear taking over. For example, here's a list of accomplishments that individual may write to remind themselves of their successes:

Coached the Little League to the championship
Implemented the office's current filing system

Installed a ceiling fan

Helped kids with homework to pass tests

Headed the ad campaign that won the best ad award

Release the need for approval

Often, our need to gain the approval of others can make a small failure seem much larger. Maybe you feel you haven't met expectations, but it's important to remind yourself that your goals are yours alone. Focus your energy on your personal goals

Accept responsibility

Failure may result from a mistake, misdirection or miscalculation. Acknowledge your role and take action to prevent further mistakes. Taking responsibility for your mistakes means accepting them and working to improve your skills and processes. By taking the time to reflect on failures and make changes to prevent them in the future, you show your accountability and willingness to grow from mistakes.

Example: Mac received a paper letter and a confirmation email stating the time and date of his licensing exam. Relying only on his memory, Mac didn't enter the appointment in his phone or on his wall calendar. As a result, Mac missed the appointment by 30 minutes and had to wait six months to test again. He acknowledged the mistake and started recording his appointments afterward.

Don't take it personally

While experiencing a business, career, or personal failure is a setback, it isn't a definition of who you are. It's easy to associate a single failure with a personal statement about you, which is why it's imperative to separate the two. Remind yourself that failure doesn't represent you as a person. You have other qualities, traits, and successes that extend beyond the mistakes you may have made. It may help to make a list of your core values and what your goals mean to you so you can motivate yourself to try again.

Channel negative emotion productively

Try to direct negative emotions toward becoming the motivation required to find a solution. Ask yourself what you could've done differently and then form an action plan to do it differently. While it's important to acknowledge how you feel after a failure, also reflect on how you can use those feelings to re-engage with your goals. Have a structured plan for reviewing your habits and processes so you can identify the source of the mistake or failure. After identifying the cause, brainstorm solutions to prevent future mistakes.

Adopt stress management skills

Practice coping skills such as deep breathing, going for a long walk, calling a friend, or spending time with your pet to help reduce stress and anxiety. When you take time to care for yourself and reduce your stress levels, it can bring clarity and perspective. Make a habit of assessing your stress levels throughout the day. If you find yourself overwhelmed, use your stress management skills to take a break.

Boost self-esteem

Failure can impact self-esteem and might elicit doubts about your ability or value. Reduce the negative impact on self-esteem by remembering that you're likely to have other opportunities in the future. Shift your attention to a hobby or low-stakes activity that you enjoy. Participating in activities that you enjoy and feel confident doing can be a great way to improve your self-esteem.

Seek support

External support can help you process and overcome failures. A friend or colleague may validate your feelings or share a story of failure that lessens the impact of yours. Family and friends may offer advice or simply provide a space to hear your thoughts aloud. Talking about your experiences and feelings is important for understanding them, alleviating their effect on you, and brainstorming solutions with trusted individuals. Additionally, it can improve your relationships with others when you ask them for support and offer support in return.

Find inspiration in your mistakes

Mistakes can be sources of inspiration that help you make other improvements in your life. For example, if you make a mistake, you may use the opportunity to develop a new method of performing the task or working toward the initial goal. Using your mistake as an opportunity to innovate and problem-solve can be a valuable experience.

Adapt to changing circumstances

It's common to overlook details when you follow a particular routine. For example, if you perform repetitive tasks in your job, you may overlook a minor detail or forget to incorporate a recent update. When changes happen in your routine, it's important to take additional time to adapt. Additionally, you may choose to change your routine occasionally to improve your focus or try tasks in a new way that may encourage creative thinking and innovation.

Find a new perspective

When experiencing a failure, consider it an opportunity to gain a new perspective. By acknowledging your feelings, practicing self-care, and evaluating your steps, you may identify new ways of thinking about your habits. Failure can be a great opportunity to evaluate your habits and thinking patterns to find new ways of approaching challenges or goals. When you think about challenges or goals from a new perspective, you may find different solutions.

Know when to progress forward

Reflecting on failures can help you know when it's time to progress forward from a task or goal. Acknowledging that the goal isn't currently achievable or doesn't align with your needs and expectations can be valuable. Releasing unrealistic or unnecessary goals through failure can help you focus your attention on other priorities that may better suit your long-term objectives. For example, if you're struggling to earn a promotion in your current workplace, you may look for other opportunities that better fit your skills, needs, and career goals.

Recovering from failure

Even high-performing athletes or teams that have a major failure. But many athletes have turned the agony of defeat into human triumph. Skater Surya Bonaly. She was a nine-time French National Champion and won the European Championship five times. Still, she failed to medal in all three of her Olympic appearances. Finishing fifth in 1992, fourth in 1994, and tenth in 1998. On retiring as a professional athlete, she worked as a figure skating coach and a motivational speaker.

Over time, you may shift your focus to feeling successful from process outcomes. The structure put forth by Atomic Habits author James Clear might be helpful to you in that case. He's identified three stages of failure:

Failure of vision is when you are not clear about what you want or your personal "why." When you don't know what you want out of life. Or if you are not feeling purpose and meaning in your life. Then you might be having a failure of vision. This is where looking inward and focusing on your well-being can make a difference.

Failure of tactics is when you know what you want but don't have a clear or effective plan for achieving it. For instance, maybe you've failed to complete a project because you only have a general sketch and not a master plan. Even those who are effective at strategic planning in the workplace sometimes struggle. Especially with translating those skills into tactics for personal or leadership development. This is where habit tracking and development can be very effective.

Failure of strategy is when you have a plan and follow it, but still do not achieve your goal. An endless number of factors could be affecting your success. They may be related or unrelated to your plan. Failure of strategy is an ideal moment to employ your design thinking skills and get working on the next iteration.

Understanding why you feel failure can help you overcome challenges to your process outcomes. Perhaps you're "simply unfinished." Then, thinking through this will result in "renewed motivation" to achieve your process outcomes. Keep in mind that none of us can avoid failure all the time. That isn't the intent. We live in a world where our success as individuals and teams depends on us learning more and faster to perform better. If we aren't failing, we probably aren't taking enough risks.

Failure is a great teacher. It can be a valuable lesson for us in the long run. We should be able to examine it and take important lessons away from it. Performing a failure analysis and looking at the root causes of our failure is a key way of learning from failure. This is particularly true if you suffer a complex failure where the reason for failure may not be immediately clear.

It's nice to know what we are doing right in our jobs or businesses. But failure feedback gives us something equally important: a learning process or teachable moment about what we are doing wrong as well. Often, small failures early on in a project can almost be like an experiment. These failures can create innovation that leads to future success.

Performing a failure analysis

There are several different frameworks that you can use for failure analysis. One of the most popular is FMEA (failure mode and effects analysis). Performing a failure analysis allows you to calculate a risk priority number (RPN) for a process. An RPN is based on the severity, occurrence rate, and detection rate of different challenges that may arise in your business processes. To perform a process failure analysis, there are 10 steps that you need to follow:

1. Review the process

2. Brainstorm potential failure modes (root causes)

3. List the potential effects of each failure

4. Assign severity rankings

5. Assign occurrence rankings

6. Assign detection rankings

7. Calculate the RPN (risk priority number)

8. Develop an action plan

9. Take action

10. Calculate the resulting RPN (risk priority number)

If you want to take a more structured approach to learn from your model, these steps will guide you through the process.

How to Avoid Failure

Denzel Washington is quoted as saying, "The two most important days in your life are, the day you're born and the day you find out WHY."

Many people wonder why failed sometimes in life without knowing exactly the reasons for these failures and how to avoid failure in general. Why have they missed so many opportunities and possibilities to improve their life? The following are the most common mistakes that are causing a lack of success.

Be committed and dedicated to 100 %! One specific thing I noticed when analyzing failures was that people didn´t show their fullest engagement with the projects or aims they were targeting. They lacked in having the necessary commitment, which resulted in them performing their work only half-assed, engendering failure and frustration. The key to completing projects extraordinarily successfully is to focus on these tasks with

> all your desire
> your fullest attention
> commitment and dedication

Avoid a lack of engagement! lack of engagement is a very important factor for failure. You will always have to bear in mind that a mission that you aren´t committed to can always fail. But once you know how to avoid failure and start to reach specific goals and aims with all your desire and energy the percentage of failings and breakdowns will be dramatically reduced.

Focus your attention! Another very common mistake that is the main reason for failure is to have a lot of different projects and goals you are trying to pursue at one time. It's always great to have aims in life, but the problem with having too many projects at one time is that you will not be able to give every project your fullest attention. This results in mental overload as well as a neglect of quality, the basic requirement for failures and collapses. Instead of trying to reach dozens of different aims, you should focus only on a few ones, but even more focused and with your fullest intention to do whatever it takes to reach these.

Avoiding stupid mistakes. Don´t give up too quickly! I have seen a lot of people setting themselves some great and ambitious goals for their lives that were inspiring for me. Unfortunately, I have also seen a lot of them neglecting their great aims and surrendering after a while. This happened often because specific obstacles showed up, causing them to abandon their goals. But isn´t it the commitment to do whatever it takes to reach a specific aim, once we have set it? It is the willingness to identify and overcome every obstacle to achieve our goals. This is what makes us successful. It is the attitude to never give up that enables us to know how to avoid failure.

Ch 7

Building Resilience Through Perseverance

In the face of life's inevitable challenges and setbacks, resilience and perseverance stand out as the key to overcoming setbacks and achieving success. Resilience refers to our ability to bounce back from adversity or change, to recover, and move forward. Perseverance is about the continued effort to achieve something despite difficulties, failure, or opposition. It's about staying the course, even when the going gets tough. Each of these qualities plays a unique role in how we navigate challenges and pursue our goals. Resilience is the ability to bounce back from adversity, while perseverance is the determination to keep going even when things get tough. Together, they form a powerful duo that can help you overcome obstacles and achieve your goals.

Resilience and perseverance play significant roles in both our personal and professional lives. They are the driving forces that propel us toward success and help us navigate the inevitable challenges and setbacks we encounter along the way. We can better recognize and cultivate these traits in ourselves and others. This, in turn, can empower us to face life's challenges more effectively, to persist in our endeavors, and ultimately, to lead more fulfilling and successful lives.

Developing resilience and perseverance traits are crucial for several reasons. They not only help us achieve our goals and overcome challenges, but they also contribute to our overall well-being. They can boost our self-confidence, improve our problem-solving skills, and enhance our ability to cope with stress and adversity. By cultivating resilience and perseverance, we can equip ourselves with the tools we need to navigate life's challenges and achieve success in all areas of our lives.

Resilience and perseverance are not just desirable qualities but essential ones. They are the driving forces that propel us toward success, help us navigate challenges, and ultimately shape our lives. By intentionally developing these traits, we equip ourselves with the tools to navigate life's challenges and achieve success in all areas of our lives. The journey may not always be easy, but with resilience, perseverance, and persistence, it is certainly possible.

Resilience and perseverance are your secret weapons as a leader. They're like the elastic waistband on your leadership pants, ready to stretch and accommodate whatever challenges come your way (figuratively, of course). It's also important to remember that failure is a natural part of the journey to success. When setbacks occur, view them as opportunities for growth and learning. Use your failures as a chance to assess your approach and make improvements.

Here are a few examples of resilience and perseverance to make it more relatable for ourselves:

The instance of airplane landing by Captain Chesley "Sully" Sullenberger. In 2009, he was piloting US Airways Flight 1549 when both engines were disabled after a bird strike shortly after take-off. With quick thinking and composure, Sullenberger safely landed the plane on the Hudson River, saving the lives of all

155 passengers and crew members on board. His calmness under pressure and ability to make split-second decisions showcased his resilience and perseverance in the face of an extraordinary challenge.

The classical examples are Elon Musk, Mary Barra, and Jeff Bezos who succeeded despite setbacks:

Elon Musk, the CEO of Tesla and SpaceX, is another leader who has demonstrated resilience and perseverance. Musk faced countless setbacks and criticisms throughout his journey of revolutionizing the electric car and space exploration industries. Despite encountering numerous obstacles, such as production delays, financial difficulties, and technical challenges, Musk continued to push forward, believing in his vision and persevering against all odds.

Mary Barra, CEO of General Motors (GM): Barra assumed leadership of GM in 2014 during a time of intense scrutiny and challenges following a major recall crisis. She implemented measures to enhance product safety and quality while fostering a culture of accountability and transparency. Barra's resilience and determination helped rebuild trust in GM and restore its reputation.

Jeff Bezos, former CEO of Amazon: Bezos founded Amazon in 1994 and faced numerous obstacles throughout the company's growth. He encountered skepticism, financial struggles, and operational challenges. However, Bezos persevered, focusing on customer satisfaction, innovation, and long-term growth strategies. His resilience and unwavering commitment to his vision led Amazon to become one of the world's most valuable companies.

These leaders serve as inspiring examples of resilience and perseverance, showcasing the importance of staying focused, determined, and adaptable in the face of adversity. Their stories remind us that great leaders are not immune to challenges but rather rise above them with unwavering determination and resilience.

Resilience and perseverance are crucial behavioral competencies when individuals and organizations must overcome significant obstacles. The capacity to be flexible as well as demonstrate the range of responses to adversity will dramatically impact our level of future success. One of senior management's responsibilities is to ensure that during these transitional times, we surround ourselves with the people who approach these challenges with the most appropriate behavioral competencies.

Resilience and perseverance are crucial behavioral competencies when individuals and organizations must overcome significant obstacles. The capacity to be flexible as well as demonstrate the range of responses to adversity will dramatically impact our level of future success. One of senior management's responsibilities is to ensure that during these transitional times, we surround ourselves with the people who approach these challenges with the most appropriate behavioral competencies.

Demonstrating resilience and perseverance

As a leader, you are bound to face challenges, setbacks, and failures. How you handle those obstacles can make all the difference in your team's success. Demonstrating resilience and perseverance is critical to achieving success. It's easy to get discouraged when facing setbacks, obstacles, and challenges, but the ability to persevere through tough times is what sets successful leaders apart. Demonstrating resilience and perseverance as a leader can help you navigate tough times and inspire your team to do the same.

One of the best ways to demonstrate resilience and perseverance as a leader is to lead by example. When you face a setback, don't give up or lose hope. Instead, take a step back and assess the situation. Look for solutions and seek advice from your team if necessary.

Communicating your plans and goals to your team is also important. When your team understands your vision and direction, they are more likely to be invested in the outcome. Encourage open communication and feedback from your team. Listen to their ideas and concerns, and work together to find solutions.

Another key aspect of demonstrating resilience and perseverance as a leader is maintaining a positive attitude. Even in the face of adversity, try to maintain a positive outlook and motivate your team to do the same. Celebrate small successes along the way, and use those wins as fuel to keep pushing forward.

Three Clues:

Stay composed in challenging situations: When faced with adversity or setbacks, maintain a calm and composed demeanor. Demonstrate emotional stability and show your team that you can handle difficult circumstances with grace and composure.

Adapt and embrace change: In a rapidly changing world, the ability to adapt is crucial. Demonstrate your resilience by embracing change and leading your team through transitions. Be flexible and open-minded, finding innovative solutions and adjusting your strategies when needed.

Communicate effectively: Clear and transparent communication is essential during times of adversity. Keep your team informed about challenges, changes, and progress. Provide guidance, support, and reassurance to help your team stay focused and motivated.

Resilience

Resilience is the capacity to recover quickly from difficulties and to bounce back from adversity or change. It's a mental and emotional toughness that allows us to maintain our equilibrium and keep moving forward in the face of hardship.

The role of resilience in life is paramount. It enables us to navigate through life's ups and downs, to adapt to change, and to learn from our failures and setbacks. Resilience is what allows us to pick ourselves up, dust ourselves off, and keep going after a fall. Real-life examples of resilience are plentiful. Consider a student who fails a major exam but uses the experience as a learning opportunity, studying harder and seeking extra help to improve. Or think of a business that suffers a significant financial loss but manages to pivot, adapt, and ultimately thrive in a new market.

In our personal lives, resilience helps us cope with personal hardships such as loss, illness, or other life changes. It allows us to bounce back from these adversities and continue moving forward. In a professional context, resilience can help us adapt to changes in the workplace, cope with job loss, or navigate career transitions. It's the trait that enables us to learn from our mistakes and failures, turning them into opportunities for growth and improvement.

When something goes wrong, do you tend to bounce back or fall apart? When you have resilience, you harness the inner strength that helps you rebound from a setback or challenge, such as a job loss, an illness, a disaster, or a loved one's death. If you lack resilience, you might get stuck on problems or feel like a victim. You might feel burdened or turn to ways to cope that aren't healthy, such as drug or alcohol use, eating disorders, or risky behaviors.

Resilience won't make your problems go away. But resilience can help you see past them, find ways to enjoy life, and better handle stress. If you aren't as resilient as you'd like to be, you can learn skills to become more resilient.

Adapting to tough times. Resilience means being able to cope with tough events. When something bad happens, you still feel anger, grief, and pain. But you're able to keep going, both physically and psychologically. Resilience isn't about putting up with something tough or coping on your own. Being able to reach out to others for support is a key part of being resilient.

Resilience and mental health. Resilience can help protect you from mental health conditions, such as depression and anxiety. Resilience also can help you deal with things that increase the risk of mental health conditions, such as being bullied or having trauma. If you have a mental health condition, being resilient can help you cope better.

There are four main types of resilience that we must cultivate to support ourselves during difficult times. These include physical resilience, mental resilience, emotional resilience, and social resilience.

1. Psychological Resilience: Psychological resilience is the mental capacity to deal with or adapt to uncertainty, difficulties, and adversity. Sometimes, it is referred to as "mental fortitude." Psychologically resilient people develop coping strategies and skills such as (problem-solving and being agile) that enable them to stay calm and focused during a crisis and move on without long-term negative consequences such as distress and anxiety.

2. Emotional Resilience: Emotional resilience refers to the various ways in which we manage our emotional responses to challenges and deal with our feelings and negative emotions such as anger, fear, vulnerability, or sadness. It is pivotal that we accept the reality of our situation while also having the emotional capacity to get through it. Understanding how we react to challenges and minimizing the impact on ourselves, and others requires emotional awareness or emotional intelligence. Emotionally resilient people comprehend their emotions and their causes. Even amid a crisis, they maintain a realistic sense of optimism and make proactive use of both internal and external resources. They can

effectively manage both external stressors and their own emotions.

3. Physical Resilience: Physical resilience refers to the body's ability to adapt effectively to physical challenges, and maintain the stamina and strength necessary to heal promptly and effectively. Physical resilience is influenced by healthy lifestyle choices, connections with friends and neighbors, deep breathing, adequate rest and recovery time, and participation in enjoyable activities.

4. Social Resilience: Social resilience refers to the capacity of a group of people to adapt to and bounce back from adversity, whether that be a natural disaster, an act of violence, or economic hardship. It is about the bonds we form with one another and our ability to lean on one another in times of need. When dealing with difficult times, it helps to have people you can lean on for moral and emotional support from your community, family, and friends. Real-life examples of community resilience include New York City after the 9/11 terrorist attacks; New Orleans following Hurricane Katrina; and the communities of Gilroy, California, El Paso, Texas, Dayton, Ohio, and Uvalde, Texas, in the aftermath of mass shootings.

While all types of resilience are important, emotional resilience is vital to our ability to remain afloat during difficult times because it directly relates to our mental health and our capacity to persevere, sustain ourselves, and manage negative reactions from those around us who are also likely to be struggling with a variety of issues.

Tips to improve your resilience

To become more resilient, try some of these tips:

Get connected. Building strong, healthy relationships with loved ones and friends can give you needed support and help guide you in good and bad times. Connect with others by volunteering or joining a faith or spiritual group.

Make every day have meaning. Do something that gives you a sense of success and purpose every day. Set clear goals that you can reach to help you look toward the future with meaning.

Learn from the past. Think of how you've coped with troubles in the past. Think about what has helped you through tough times. You can even write about past events in a journal to help you see the patterns of how you behave and to help guide you in the future.

Stay hopeful. You can't change the past, but you can always look toward the future. Being open to change makes it easier to adapt and view new challenges with less worry.

Take care of yourself. Tend to your own needs and feelings. Do activities and hobbies you enjoy. Include physical activity in your daily routine. Get plenty of sleep and make bedtime rituals. Eat a healthy diet. Practice how to manage stress. Try ways to relax, such as yoga, meditation, guided imagery, deep breathing, or prayer.

Take action. Don't ignore your problems. Instead, figure out what you need to do, make a plan, and take action. It can take time to recover from a major setback, trauma, or loss. But know that your life can improve if you work at it.

Perseverance

Perseverance is keeping going even though you want to stop, or it's bouncing back from failure to try again. There may be good reasons for quitting something, and the right time to do so, but psychologists studying the concept of "grit" found that the capacity to stick with a task — particularly when faced with difficulties — is a crucial factor in explaining success.

There are other good reasons to persevere. Persevering in the face of challenges can help you reach a particular goal, but it can also mean that you will likely learn new skills along the way to that goal. And Stanford Psychology professor Carol Dweck's work has found that by persevering you will become a better performer in the long term, having more success every time you reach for a goal.

You have goals and dreams. You have faced rejections and obstacles that have knocked you down more times than you can count. But you're still standing. Why? Because you have something deep within you that refuses to give up. There are two characteristics responsible for your ability to withstand difficulties and push on against the odds: perseverance and resilience.

Perseverance is your ability to persist against challenges and maintain your effort and action over the long haul. Perseverance is the continued effort to do or achieve something despite difficulties, failure, or opposition. It's about staying the course, and remaining committed to our goals, even when the going gets tough. Perseverance plays a crucial role in achieving our goals. It's the fuel that keeps us going when we're faced with obstacles or when progress seems slow. Without perseverance, we're likely to give up at the first sign of difficulty. Examples of perseverance abound in every field. Consider the athlete who trains diligently every day, despite injuries or losses, to improve their performance. Or the scientist who conducts hundreds of experiments, undeterred by repeated failures, until they finally make a breakthrough.

Perseverance is crucial when we're working towards personal goals, whether it's pursuing a hobby, improving a relationship, or maintaining a healthy lifestyle. It's the quality that keeps us going, even when progress is slow or obstacles arise. In the workplace, perseverance can mean the difference between giving up on a challenging project and seeing it through to completion. It's what drives us to keep striving for success, even in the face of difficulties or setbacks.

Perseverance is the ability to persist in the face of obstacles or discouragement. It's continuing a course of action without giving up in the face of difficulties or opposition. Perseverance means dogged determination and the will to push on when the going gets tough. The persevering person says, "I will find a way."

Examples of Perseverance: Throughout history, there have been countless examples of perseverance in the face of adversity. Individuals who refuse to give up in pursuit of their goals and dreams, no matter the obstacles, serve as inspiration and motivation for us all. To sit a few:

1. The famous inventor *Thomas Edison* persevered through over 10,000 failed attempts at creating the first commercially viable lightbulb. His numerous unsuccessful tries did not deter him. He viewed each attempt as bringing him closer to success. His perseverance and determination eventually paid off, and he went on to obtain over 1,000 patents in his lifetime.

2. Nelson Mandela persevered through 27 years of imprisonment for fighting against apartheid in South Africa. Despite the brutal conditions, he never gave up hope. He continued to stand up for what he believed in, even from his prison cell. His perseverance and commitment to justice and equality helped bring an end to apartheid and shaped him into an iconic leader and human rights champion.

3. At just 19 months old, Helen Keller lost her sight and hearing due to illness. But with the help of her teacher, Annie Sullivan, she persevered against immense challenges to learn how to communicate. She went on to become the first deaf-blind person to earn a Bachelor of Arts degree, becoming an acclaimed author and activist. Her perseverance in the face of seemingly insurmountable obstacles serves as an inspiration to all.

The efforts and determination of individuals like Edison, Mandela, and Keller highlight the power of human perseverance. Their stories remind us that we are capable of overcoming immense adversity and achieving great things, as long as we refuse to give up in the face of failures and setbacks. Perseverance is a skill we can all develop, and these examples shine a light on its ability to change the world.

Strategies for Building Resilience

Practice Optimism: Try to maintain a positive outlook even in difficult situations. This doesn't mean ignoring the negative, but rather acknowledging it and then focusing on potential solutions or next steps.

Embrace Change: Accept that change is a part of life and try to adapt to new situations. This flexibility can help build resilience.

Develop Problem-Solving Skills: Instead of avoiding problems, face them head-on and work to find solutions. This proactive approach can enhance resilience.

Build Strong Relationships: Having a strong support network can provide emotional support and practical help when facing adversity, thereby strengthening resilience.

Strategies for Building Perseverance

How to Persevere?

Once you are clear that you want to persevere — you've made sure your goals are worth pursuing and carefully considered that your goals pose no unnecessary damage to your health, relationships, or the like — consider the following strategies to help you persevere:

Recall past perseverance. Bringing to mind past instances when you persisted can help strengthen your resolve and give you energy, focus, and determination to persevere now. Think about the last time you felt fierce, strong, stubborn, unyielding, clear, inspired, surrendered, on a mission, purposeful, focused, or committed. Remember it, feel it in your body, and bring it to mind when you feel you need resources to keep going.

Take a step, even just a small one. Identify one small thing you can do right now to make progress toward your goal. There usually is something that can be done. Identifying immediately actionable tasks and completing one is more beneficial than getting stressed about all the things that need to happen in the future to meet your goal. Take the available steps; this will bring the next steps into reach and give you a boost for having made progress.

Set a reasonable pace. Work and make progress towards your goals, but avoid frenzied activity or panicked states of mind that will just burn you out. "Slow and steady wins the race!"

Try other solutions. If you're stuck, make sure you've explored your options for other ways of accomplishing your goal or getting through your next step. It can sometimes be helpful to brainstorm with others — a friend, adviser, family member, or counselor — about possible solutions.

Be patient and give things time. Don't forget that things take time. Dreams aren't fulfilled overnight, so don't get discouraged if things aren't happening quickly enough. If you've just embarked on an effort, it's especially important to give the effort time so that you don't let the newness of it scare you off.

Just keep going (even if it's only in your mind). Remember that your efforts will pay off by putting one foot in front of the other. And if you're truly stuck and can't move forward (because you are sick, or blocked waiting on some external change), keep your spirits up. Know that being intent on your goal, and not giving up, is progress in itself. You can take comfort in these lovely and self-compassionate words of wisdom by best—selling author and psychologist Dr. Rick Hanson, "*You can continue to reflect on what's happening, learn to cope with it better, and love the people around you. And over time maybe things will improve.*"

Set Clear Goals: Having a clear goal in mind gives you something to strive for and can help fuel your perseverance.

Break Down Goals: Large goals can seem overwhelming. Break them down into smaller, manageable tasks to make them seem less daunting.

Celebrate Small Wins: Recognize and celebrate progress, no matter how small. This can boost your motivation and help you persevere.

Practice Patience: Understand that progress takes time and that setbacks are a part of the process. Patience can help you stay the course and persevere.

Steps to have Resilience and Perseverance

We all face our own unique set of difficult circumstances. Some of us have exercised our resilience muscles more than others.

1. Relationships

We can all identify critical people in our lives. But when building relationships, we have to know who the right people are to make a relationship. We all hear frightening stories relating to relationships in our societies. For some, it takes years to realize that it is not worth it to keep certain relationships, be it social, personal, or professional.

One of the most important relationships we have is with the Divine. Of course, not everyone has God as an emphasis in their life. One universal relationship is the relationship with ourselves. It would be superb if we were kind and accepting of who we are. We should also surround ourselves with compassionate and empathetic people. It is good to have a support group, even if only one or two correct key people.

2. Self-Care

Wellness in self-care isn't just a trendy fad; it is essential to maintaining good physical and mental health and building resilience. Positive lifestyle choices like good nutrition, proper exercise, plenty of water, and adequate rest can help keep our body and mind ready for whatever happens in life.

Practice mindfulness through journaling, prayer or meditation, or yoga and breathing exercises. These simple practices can help us be prepared to cope with difficult situations. It can help us develop more gratitude. And gratitude has a significant impact on your resilience.

Avoid negative outlets that can be self-destructive, like negative self-talk, anger, jealousy smoking, drugs, or alcohol. These substances can mask pain, but they will never solve our problems.

3. De-stress

Stress is something that every human experiences at some point in their life. Sometimes, stress is necessary to push us to grow. When we stress out, let's take time to reflect on what caused the stress. Was it a situation where we were forced into action or did, we create the situation by taking on too much responsibility?

Identify signs of stress that are building in our lives. Signs of stress are unique and can manifest both physically and emotionally. Some examples might include muscle tension or weakness, restlessness, and even exhaustion, or digestion problems. Emotionally we might experience anxiety, sadness, irritability, or become short-tempered with others. If we can identify sources of stress in our lives, we can better decrease or manage stress.

Create a stress-free environment where one can find renewed strength. This stress-free environment could be a comfortable environment like a park or an experience like reading a book or taking a walk. It is vital to address stress as soon as possible to prevent chronic stress from becoming the norm.

4. Identify Purpose

Many of the people I know seem to have a deep sense of purpose. Working for simply anything in life they've found ways to blend their passion, talents, and care for the world in a way that infuses their lives with meaning. Luckily for some, having a purpose in life is associated with all kinds of benefits. Research suggests that purpose is tied to having better health, longevity, and even economic success. It feels good to have a sense of purpose, knowing that you are using your skills to help others in a way that matters to you.

5. Start Forgiving

The final step of building resilience is all about forgiveness. This is a major piece because it becomes difficult to endure new challenges when we hang onto the difficulties we have endured. This can have a considerable impact on our daily life.

Besides forgiving, we need to accept forgiveness. The previous failure is something we all know, and it's okay to let it go. When we apply these simple steps to our lives, we will become much more resilient to this, I'm sure. Besides these steps, we can do some other things when encouraging children to be resilient.

Ways You Can Improve Your Perseverance Skills

Everyone in life has setbacks, both big and small. The bigger ones may feel more noticeable, but even the smaller ones can take a toll on the way we think and feel. These challenges can leave people scrambling to keep up and might lead to people reconsidering their paths and goals.

1. Don't be afraid to fail.

Perseverance comes from failing and getting back up. Without failure, you cannot become resilient. So you have to change your relationship with failure to see it as a lesson, rather than a setback. You can learn so much from failure that changing your attitude toward it can have amazing implications for your life.

2. Be 1% better every day.

Having a growth mindset is a great way to increase perseverance and motivation. Understand that these are skills like any other and try to improve upon them by just 1% every day. Keeping this concept at the back of your head throughout the day is a great way to get better in all regards.

3. Begin to take risks.

By learning to take risks, you raise the probability of facing more difficult situations. When in those difficult situations, if you can learn to adapt and understand what steps are necessary to keep the company moving in the right direction, you can grow as a leader.

4. Understand resistance.

More people can persevere when they have a better understanding of resistance. Every business owner who struggles with it should read The War of Art by Steven Pressfield. This book helps one be able to identify what it is that tries to hold them back. When one can name the resistance, it loses its power and there is more room for perseverance.

5. Exercise regularly.

Apply the 40% rule. The rule is that if you complete 40% of the task, your likelihood of quitting drops drastically. I believe that the No. 1 way to develop this skill is physical training. Lifting weights, doing sprints or even some endurance training is guaranteed to carry over to your mental resilience.

6. Build a network of support.

If you want to learn how to persevere, you should build a network of support. Building a network of support that includes family, friends, co-workers, and peers will allow you to have a comfortable place to open up and get feedback and encouragement during hard times. Whenever something goes wrong, you can turn to your network of support and talk through what's going on.

7. Keep your goals in mind.

When we make mistakes or fail, many people will be tempted to give up altogether. Instead, if you want to persevere, keep your goals in mind at all times. Start by writing down your short and long-term goals somewhere that's easy to access. Then, anytime there's a bump in the road, take a look at that list to inspire you and keep you moving forward.

8. Set clear benchmarks.

Success can be a long and tough journey. I suggest instilling benchmarks to provide yourself with rewards or encouragement along the way. The rewards can be anything from a fancy lunch to new clothes or a weekend vacation. The benchmarks will keep reminding you of the progress you have made. Additionally, the reward helps provide continued motivation to persevere through difficult times.

9. Remember your 'why.'

Getting a break from doing anything in this world can be tough. I was once told by an old professor, "It's not the most talented people that make it, it's the ones with the most endurance." And that is true. For me, I have to remember the "why." Why am I doing this? What was the original reason I set out on this path? Reflecting on that reminds me that this journey is worth my time.

Chapter 8

Leveraging Failure

for Innovative Solutions

"Failure comes part and parcel with invention. It is not optional. We understand that and believe in failing early and iterating until we get it right." - **Jeff Bezos,** Founder and executive chairman of Amazon

Not all failures can, or should, be avoided. When you think of the most pivotal lessons in your life, are they from your biggest wins or easiest days? The fact is that the greatest lessons of life come from some of the darkest and most challenging times. The pain and frustration of failure imprint on us in a way that success cannot. Yes, it hurts, but it also offers us an opportunity to leverage the lesson for our gain.

Innovation is not a linear path paved with unbroken successes. Instead, it's a complex maze where dead ends, detours, and setbacks are not just common but necessary. Thomas Edison's quest to invent the electric light bulb exemplifies this, as he famously stated, "I have not failed. I've just found 10,000 ways that won't work." Each failed attempt is a lesson, a valuable piece of information that guides innovators closer to their goal. By redefining failure as a learning opportunity rather than a defeat, innovators can cultivate resilience and adaptability, essential traits for navigating the uncertain terrain of innovation.

Creativity thrives in environments where risks are encouraged and failures are viewed as progress. Google's principle of "failing fast" illustrates this mindset, where rapid prototyping and iterative development are employed to test ideas quickly and learn from failures early in the process. This approach fosters a culture of experimentation, where unconventional ideas are tested, and failures are seen as stepping stones to innovative solutions.

Failed innovations are the process. History is replete with examples of failed innovations that paved the way for groundbreaking advancements. The story of Xerox PARC, where pioneering technologies like the graphical user interface were initially deemed failures, only to later revolutionize personal computing, is a testament to the latent potential in failed experiments. Similarly, the initial rejection of digital photography, developed by Kodak, underscores the importance of recognizing and adapting to failure's hidden opportunities.

While innovation necessitates a certain degree of risk and acceptance of failure, the margin for error in critical systems is negligible. The challenge lies in finding a balance where the lessons of failure can be leveraged without compromising on the safety and reliability of engineering outcomes. However, when we dissect failures only after the fact, we miss the point that failure is not a discrete event to be analyzed in hindsight, but rather an integral part of the creative process. It is a continuous feedback loop that, when properly integrated, propels forward movement and evolution.

An ecosystem that embraces failure is key to sustaining innovation. This involves creating organizational cultures that encourage risk-taking and view failures as essential elements of the innovation process. Companies like SpaceX exemplify this, where spectacular failures in rocket launches are openly analyzed and used as learning experiences to perfect future missions.

Changing mindsets to see the identification of what does not work as a success is essential for teams to embrace innovation failure. Imagine if researchers published failed experiments? Imagine how much time would be saved by other researchers simply replicating the same failed results. It could be argued that innovation and successes would be made faster if knowledge sharing of failures was made available.

How to leverage failure from oneself:

1 Adopt a growth mindset

A growth mindset is the belief that you can improve your abilities and skills through effort, practice, and learning. A growth mindset helps you see failure as a challenge, not a threat. It also helps you focus on the process, not the outcome, and appreciate the value of effort, not just talent. A growth mindset fosters curiosity, resilience, and optimism, which are essential for creativity and innovation. To adopt a growth mindset, you need to replace fixed and limiting beliefs with flexible and empowering ones. For example, instead of thinking "I'm not good at this", think "I can learn to do this better".

2 Embrace feedback

Feedback is a vital source of information and guidance for any creative and innovative project. Feedback helps you identify your strengths and weaknesses, improve your performance, and refine your ideas. However, feedback can also trigger negative emotions and defensive reactions, especially when you perceive it as criticism or rejection. To embrace feedback, you need to overcome your ego and fear of failure and seek constructive and diverse feedback from different sources. You also need to listen actively, ask clarifying questions, and thank the feedback giver. Most importantly, you need to act on the feedback and apply it to your project.

3 Experiment and iterate

Experimentation and iteration are key methods for testing and validating your ideas, as well as generating new ones. Experimentation involves trying out different approaches, hypotheses, and prototypes, and observing the results. Iteration involves making changes and improvements based on the feedback and data from the experiments. Experimentation and iteration allow you to learn from failure, rather than avoid it. They also help you to adapt to changing conditions, discover new opportunities, and optimize your solutions. To experiment and iterate effectively, you need to plan your experiments, measure your outcomes, and document your learnings.

4 Leverage your strengths and passions

Your strengths and passions are the sources of your unique value and contribution to any creative and innovative project. Your strengths are the things that you are good at and enjoy doing, while your passions are the things that you care about and find meaningful. Leveraging your strengths and passions helps you to overcome failure because they give you confidence, motivation, and satisfaction. They also help you to create original and authentic solutions that resonate with your audience and stakeholders. To leverage your strengths and passions, you need to identify them, align them with your goals, and apply them to your project.

5 Here's what else to consider

This is a space to share examples, stories, or insights that don't fit into any of the previous sections. What else would you like to add?

Tips for leveraging failure to drive creativity and innovation in the workplace.

One of the first steps to encourage your team to use failure as a stepping stone to innovation and creativity is to acknowledge and celebrate failure as a valuable part of the process. Instead of hiding or blaming failures, make them visible and transparent, and recognize the efforts and insights behind them. A way to encourage your team to use failure as a stepping stone to innovation and creativity is to share and spread the lessons from failure across the organization and beyond. Rather than keeping the learnings from failure within your team or your department, leverage them as a source of knowledge and inspiration for others. You can do this by creating platforms and channels for your team to share their stories and insights from failure, such as a blog, a podcast, or a webinar. You can also collaborate and network with other teams and external partners who are interested in learning from failure, and exchange best practices and feedback.

Another way to encourage your team to use failure as a stepping stone to innovation and creativity is to model and inspire a growth mindset in yourself and your team. A growth mindset is the belief that abilities and talents can be developed through effort, feedback, and learning, rather than being fixed or innate.

To effectively integrate failure into the innovation process, leaders can adopt several specific strategies. These strategies not only help in normalizing failure but also in leveraging it as a crucial component of learning and progress. The project team is being led to embrace fear.

By focusing on following consolidated strategies, managers can effectively integrate failure into the innovation process, leading to a more resilient, adaptable, and ultimately successful team dynamic:

Don't Be Afraid to Take Risks

Creativity often entails moving past your comfort zone. While you don't want to take risks that could potentially cripple your business, risk-taking is a necessary ingredient of innovation and growth. Therefore, providing an environment where it's encouraged can be highly beneficial.

Don't Punish Failure

Provide your team with the freedom to innovate without fear of reprisal if their ideas don't work. Some of the best innovations in history were the product of many failures. View failure as an opportunity to learn and improve for the future rather than defeat.

Provide the Resources Necessary to Innovate

While it can be tempting to simply tell your team to innovate, creativity is more than just a state of mind. If your colleagues have the opportunity to be creative, you need to provide the resources to promote innovation. Whether that entails a financial investment, tools, or training materials, it's in your best interest to invest in your team to produce innovative results.

Don't Try to Measure Results Too Quickly

If an innovative idea doesn't produce desirable results within a few months, you may consider discarding it entirely. Doing so could result in a lost opportunity because some ideas take longer to yield positive outcomes.

Patience is an important element of creativity, so don't try to measure results too quickly. Give your team the freedom to improve and experiment without the pressure of strict time constraints.

Maintain an Open Mind

One of the most important components of an environment that fosters creativity and innovation is keeping an open mind. Innovation requires constantly working against your biases. Continually ask questions, be open to the answers you receive, and don't require fully conceptualized ideas before proceeding with innovation.

Foster Collaboration

Collaborative environments are vital for innovation. When teams work together in pursuit of a common goal, innovation flourishes. To achieve this, ensure everyone has a voice. One way to do so is by hosting brainstorming sessions where each member contributes and shares ideas.

Encourage Diversity

Diversity fosters creativity and combats groupthink, as each individual brings a unique outlook to the table. Consider forming teams with members from different cultural backgrounds who haven't previously worked together. Getting people to step outside their comfort zones is an effective way to encourage innovation.

Foster a Safe-to-Fail Environment

Create a culture where team members feel comfortable taking calculated risks and experimenting, knowing that failures are not penalized but seen as learning opportunities. Utilizing simulations and prototypes to test ideas in a risk-free environment can allow engineers to explore innovative solutions without the immediate pressure of real-world consequences.

Rapid Prototyping, Incremental Advancement, and Continuous Feedback

Emphasize rapid prototyping and iterative testing, and combine this with regular retrospectives and post-mortems. This approach allows teams to learn quickly from mistakes, adjust strategies early, and continuously gather feedback to guide project development. Adopting an approach of incremental changes rather than radical leaps can help in managing risks more effectively. This method allows for gradual improvements and learning from small-scale failures.

Give Recognition to Failures and Learnings

Recognize instances where failure led to valuable insights or strategic pivots. Share these stories within the team or organization to highlight the positive outcomes of embracing failure. Connect a failure to a pivot point in product development that would not have been made possible without knowledge of failure. Leaders should publicly acknowledge when failures lead to valuable insights or contribute to learning.

Encourage Autonomy and Balance
Experimentation with Realistic Expectations

Give team members the autonomy to make decisions and balance innovative experimentation with realistic project goals and expectations. Motivate your team to take calculated risks by tying experimentation to specific goals or outcomes. This approach focuses on purposeful innovation rather than change for change's sake. Be willing to adapt goals and expectations based on what is learned through experimentation. This flexibility shows that the organization values practical insights over rigid planning.

Chapter 9

Flexibility and Adaptability

Flexibility is the ability to change one's behavior in response to different situations. This means that an individual can respond appropriately to any given circumstance. It's an essential skill for any successful person, as it allows them to adjust and make the most of their skills and knowledge.

Adaptability, on the other hand, is the ability to adjust to changing conditions or circumstances. It's a necessary skill for anyone navigating a world that is constantly undergoing rapid change. Being able to adapt to different environments, handle stress, and learn quickly are all attributes of a successful individual.

It's worth noting that flexibility and adaptability mean different things to different people. It's important to be aware of your strengths and weaknesses and how they can help you succeed. For example, if you are naturally a flexible and adaptable person, you may be well-suited to a career in sales or customer service, where you can quickly respond to customer demands and changing environments.

Ultimately, having the ability to be flexible and adaptive is a priceless attribute that can help you remain agile and successful in this ever-changing world. Whether you're looking to excel in your career or just make the most out of life, having these skills can open up many opportunities and help you reach new heights.

In today's ever-evolving workplace, it's essential to stay competitive and productive by continuously learning new skills and adapting to different tools and technologies. To succeed as an employee, you must have the ability to work in different environments, adjust to changes quickly, problem-solve, multitask, and communicate effectively.

Rigidity and inflexibility are the refusal to consider new ideas or approaches. This can be a major barrier to progress, as it prevents businesses from adapting to changing conditions. Complacency is another obstacle, as it involves staying content with the status quo and not striving for improvement.

Workplace flexibility and adaptability

Creating a culture of flexibility and adaptability is crucial to the success of any organization. It's important to remember that the workplace is constantly changing and evolving. Employees must be able to stay up to date on new tools and technologies, learn new skills, adapt to different environments, adjust to change quickly, solve problems, multitask, and communicate effectively to remain competitive and productive.

We all know that flexibility and adaptability are important traits for success in the modern workplace. Let's look at the benefits of flexibility and adaptability. Increased productivity is one of the most obvious advantages - with flexible and adaptable individuals able to adjust their approach to changing circumstances, they can find solutions and progress more quickly. Flexibility and adaptability can also help to create a more positive work environment, as employees feel supported and appreciated. In addition, flexible and adaptable people are better equipped to make decisions quickly and accurately, as they can take advantage of a range of perspectives and viewpoints. Finally, flexible and adaptable individuals are more likely to be creative and innovative, as they can think unconventionally and develop unique solutions.

Overall, flexibility and adaptability are invaluable skills in the workplace. By understanding the benefits and drawbacks of these skills, you can ensure that you are making the most of them in your daily work life. Staying competitive in the modern business environment requires flexibility and adaptability. However, many pitfalls can prevent businesses from achieving this goal. Rigidity and inflexibility, complacency, obsolescence, poor decision-making, lack of collaboration, poor communication, and focusing on short-term goals are all pitfalls that can lead to failure.

In today's competitive business landscape, organizations must be able to constantly adapt and evolve to remain competitive. The key to success is having a culture of flexibility and adaptability. Here are some tips for creating a culture of flexibility and adaptability in your organization.

First, encourage creativity and innovation among your employees. Allow them to come up with new ideas and take risks. This will help to create an environment of experimentation and growth.

Next, utilize technology to help streamline processes and make them more efficient. This will help to reduce the amount of time and effort needed to complete tasks and help your organization stay competitive.

Third, create clear goals and objectives that are easily understood and achievable. This will help employees stay focused and motivated. It will also help to ensure that the team is working towards the same goals.

Fourth, establish a rewards system to recognize and motivate employees who demonstrate flexibility and adaptability. This will help to encourage a culture of experimentation and innovation.

Fifth, provide training and development opportunities to ensure that employees have the necessary skills to be flexible and adaptable. This will help to ensure that your staff is prepared to handle any changes that may arise.

Sixth, involve employees in decision-making processes to get their input and feedback. This will help to ensure that decisions are made that are in the best interest of the organization.

Seventh, monitor progress and take corrective action when needed. This will help to ensure that your organization is always moving in the right direction.

Finally, promote open communication and collaboration to foster a culture of trust and respect. This will help to create an environment where employees feel comfortable taking initiative and experimenting with new ideas.

Chapter 10[edit fully]

Failure's Role in Development

Failure is not the end, it's just a bend in the road. It's an opportunity to learn, grow, and pivot in a new direction. So, don't be afraid, as the saying goes, 'fall seven times, stand up eight.' Keep pushing forward, and eventually, you'll reach success - and maybe even have a good laugh about the bumps along the way.

Failure is a word that often carries negative connotations, evoking feelings of disappointment, frustration, and defeat. However, when viewed through a different lens, failure can be the key to achieving mastery in any domain. Many successful individuals attribute their triumphs to the valuable lessons learned from their failures.

Sir James Dyson, the inventor of the Dyson vacuum cleaner, experienced thousands of failed prototypes before achieving success. He viewed each failure as a learning experience, continually iterating and improving upon his designs until he achieved his goal. Dyson's journey to success was not a smooth one. He faced countless setbacks and disappointments, but he never let failure deter him. Instead, he embraced it as an essential part of the development process.

Real-life case studies further illustrate the transformative power of failure. Take, for example, Thomas Edison, who famously said, "I have not failed. I've just found 10,000 ways that won't work." His persistence and ability to embrace failure ultimately led to the invention of the practical incandescent light bulb. Edison's tireless experimentation and willingness to learn from his mistakes paved the way for one of the most significant technological advancements in history.

Similarly, J.K. Rowling, author of the Harry Potter series, faced numerous rejections before finding a publisher. Her resilience in the face of failure eventually led to the creation of one of the most beloved book series of all time. Rowling's journey to success was marked by countless moments of self-doubt and rejection, but she never gave up on her dreams. Instead, she used failure as fuel to push herself harder and prove her critics wrong.

Failure is not something to be feared or avoided; it is a necessary stepping stone on the path to success. It teaches us valuable lessons, forces us to reevaluate our approach, and builds character. Without failure, we would never truly appreciate the taste of victory. So, the next time you encounter failure, embrace it with open arms and see it as an opportunity for growth and development.

The Risk of Aversion

While failure can be viewed as a necessary part of the learning process, many individuals develop a fear of failure that stifles their growth and potential. The aversion to failure often stems from societal pressures and the fear of judgment from others. Unfortunately, this aversion can lead to stagnation and missed opportunities for personal and professional development.

When individuals avoid taking risks or trying new things for fear of failure, they limit their potential for growth and progress. Stagnation sets in, and a stagnant mindset prevents individuals from exploring uncharted territories and discovering their true capabilities. They become trapped in their comfort zones, unwilling to step outside and embrace the challenges and uncertainties that come with failure.

The fear of failure can create a vicious cycle. When individuals avoid failure at all costs, they deprive themselves of the valuable lessons and experiences that failure brings. As a result, their skills and abilities stagnate, leaving them ill-equipped to navigate future challenges and adapt to changing circumstances.

Stagnation Consequences

One consequence of stagnation is the missed opportunities for personal growth. When individuals are too afraid to step outside their comfort zones, they deny themselves the chance to discover new interests, talents, and passions. By avoiding failure, they limit their ability to explore different paths and find fulfillment in areas they may have never considered before.

Stagnation can have a detrimental impact on professional development. In today's rapidly changing world, adaptability and resilience are crucial skills for success. However, individuals who are averse to failure often struggle to adapt to new technologies, trends, and ways of working. They become stuck in outdated practices and miss out on opportunities for career advancement.

Another consequence of the fear of failure is the impact on creativity and innovation. When individuals are too afraid to take risks, they shy away from exploring new ideas and pushing boundaries. Innovation requires a willingness to experiment and embrace failure as a stepping stone towards success. Without this mindset, individuals miss out on the chance to make groundbreaking discoveries and contribute to the advancement of their field.

The fear of judgment from others can lead to a lack of self-confidence and self-esteem. When individuals constantly worry about what others will think of their failures, they become hesitant to take action and express their true selves. This self-doubt can hinder personal relationships, professional growth, and overall happiness.

The aversion to failure can create a culture of conformity and mediocrity. When individuals are too focused on avoiding failure, they tend to play it safe and follow the status quo. This conformity stifles creativity, innovation, and progress. It prevents individuals from challenging the norm, questioning assumptions, and striving for excellence.

The fear of failure and aversion to taking risks can have significant consequences on personal and professional development. Stagnation, missed opportunities, limited growth, and a lack of innovation are just a few of the outcomes of this mindset. It is essential to recognize the value of failure as a learning opportunity and embrace the challenges that come with it. By doing so, individuals can unlock their true potential and lead fulfilling and successful lives.

Reframing Techniques

To overcome the aversion to failure and harness its transformative power, it is essential to adopt a growth mindset and reframe the concept of failure. By reframing failure, individuals can shift their perspective, viewing it not as a setback or defeat, but as an opportunity for growth and learning. Here are some reframing techniques that can help in this process:

The 5 Whys

The "5 Whys" is a simple yet effective technique for analyzing failures and uncovering the root causes. When faced with failure, ask yourself "why" five times to delve deeper into the underlying reasons. By repeatedly questioning and seeking to understand the underlying causes, you can identify patterns, uncover misconceptions, and develop strategies to overcome similar challenges in the future.

For example, let's say you failed to meet a deadline at work. Instead of beating yourself up over the failure, start by asking yourself *why you missed the deadline*. Perhaps you realize that you underestimated the time required for a certain task. Then, ask yourself *why you underestimated the time*. Maybe you didn't have all the necessary information to accurately estimate the effort involved. Keep asking "why" until you reach the root cause of the failure.

Once you have identified the root cause, you can take proactive steps to address it. In this case, you could improve your time management skills, gather more information before making estimates, or seek help from colleagues to ensure accurate planning. The key is to view failure as an opportunity for learning and growth, rather than dwelling on the negative aspects.

It is crucial to embrace a growth mindset, which is the belief that intelligence and abilities can be developed through effort and perseverance. By adopting this mindset, individuals can view failure as an opportunity for growth rather than a reflection of their inherent worth or capabilities.

When faced with failure, individuals with a growth mindset see it as a temporary setback, a chance to learn from mistakes and improve. They understand that failure is not a measure of their worth or intelligence but rather a stepping stone towards success. This mindset allows individuals to bounce back from failure more quickly and continue to strive for excellence.

Failure is an integral part of the journey toward mastery. Rather than avoiding failure, individuals should embrace it as a stepping stone to success. By reframing failure, developing a growth mindset, and actively seeking out growth opportunities, individuals can unlock their true potential and pave the way for personal and professional mastery.

Here are five reasons to embrace failure professionally or personally and to leverage your failures to fuel growth:

Encourages Innovation: When you let your team fail, it encourages innovation as they learn from their mistakes and find new ways to approach the problem.

Builds Resilience: Failure helps team members build resilience and learn to bounce back from setbacks. They learn to handle pressure, cope with uncertainty, and develop a growth mindset.

Promotes Learning: Failure can be an incredible learning opportunity that helps to create a culture of continuous learning where team members feel comfortable taking risks and trying new things.

Enhances Ownership: Team members are more likely to take ownership of their decisions and actions when they know failure is possible.

Fosters Trust: When you let your team fail, you demonstrate that you trust them to learn and grow from their experiences.

Reframe your perspective on failure: Rather than seeing failure as a negative, view it as an opportunity for growth and learning. Recognize that failure is an inevitable part of the process and a necessary step towards success.

Analyze the failure: Take a step back and examine what went wrong. Identify the areas where you fell short and the factors that contributed to the failure. Use this analysis to develop an improvement plan.

Embrace the learning: Use the lessons you've learned from your failure to improve your approach moving forward. Look for ways to apply the knowledge and experience gained from the failure to future challenges.

Focus on your strengths: Recognize your strengths and how they can help you overcome obstacles. Build on your strengths and leverage them to improve your performance.

Take action: Use the insights gained from the failure to make changes and take action. Implement the lessons learned and make adjustments to your approach as needed.

Embracing Change

The best learning comes from failures rather than successes. We need to change even when we are successful as success is also not permanent if we don't change based on the environment and changing dynamics in the world. Hence embracing change and learning from failures & using them as stepping stones for success is key for both personal prosperity & peace and professional success.

In nowadays business environment, where everything from technology to customer needs and business tools change constantly, you only have two options: either disrupt your industry, bringing about the change yourself; or stay alert and adapt quickly to the changes happening around you. Either way, change can work for you if you come to terms with the fact that it is there. Once you've accepted it, you can build upon that and learn how to use it to your advantage.

This is what, the movies and TV provider Netflix did almost 20 years ago before the Internet was that widespread, in 1997. It introduced a DVD video subscription rental by mail, which soon took over clients' preferences forcing all sorts of companies, including thousands of video stores, to close down and slowly disappear. It changed the whole industry by introducing a new distribution channel that people quickly embraced.

All the same, companies that ignore change can be hurt by it, even if they are leaders in their industry. It seems to be particularly difficult to embrace change for successful companies. This is what happened to Kodak. Even though they invented the digital camera, they were so focused on their film business which was thriving, that they ignored the digitalisation. Their competitors however didn't and Kodak was soon left behind, turning from a leader in their industry to just one of the many companies.

Change can be as much of a threat as it is an opportunity if you spot it and act on it, or if you proactively look for ways to get your business to evolve and move in a direction where you think the future is. Dealing with change is a daunting task because it is in our nature to not like change. However, change can be a winning move, especially for small businesses which are so much more flexible and easier to maneuver. It is much easier to initiate change than to simply react to it feeling threatened. Don't expect to be ready to dive into all sorts of changes overnight. Below are a few tips for you that might make it easier for you to learn to exploit change.

Why embracing change is crucial for your success?

We avoid it, we fear it and often we downright hate it. Change is a dirty word in the dictionary for many of us. It turns our lives around; it challenges the status quo and with it our sense of stability too. It drags us out of our comfort zone. But like it or not, change has always been and will always be a part of our lives, private or business.

Especially today, when change really is the only one constant and it takes over so rapidly in certain areas of life and business that it makes your head spin. Either way, change can work for you if you come to terms with the fact that it is there. Once you've accepted it, you can build upon that and learn how to use it to your advantage.

This is what, the movies and TV provider Netflix did almost 20 years ago before the Internet was that widespread, in 1997. It introduced a DVD video subscription rental by mail, which soon took over clients' preferences forcing all sorts of companies, including thousands of video stores, to close down and slowly disappear. It changed the whole industry by introducing a new distribution channel that people quickly embraced. All the same, companies that ignore change can be hurt by it, even if they are leaders in their industry.

Think about possible changes in your business. Chances are you are probably comfortable with the way you do business now, your processes, your procedures, your offerings, your marketing tools, etc. And that is because you are so used to it. Sit down and brainstorm, and get your colleagues and employees to come up with different ideas. You don't want to be changing things all the time but you do need to do it sometimes. Think, read, stay informed about what is happening in your industry, and stir things up now and then. You never know, you might be the one bringing about the next big change in your industry, which of course gives you an edge.

Take small steps. Think about where you want to get and work backward breaking it down into small steps. Start with the small changes that you can make today and that will eventually lead you to what you want to achieve.

Be open & positive. When people see that you are confident and optimistic, chances are they too will feel positive. Furthermore, once you involve people and get them to come up with ideas themselves, this will improve the work morale and motivation and thus their commitment to making the changes happen.

There's always a chance that your new idea proves to be not so great and you fail. It is not a nice feeling, but let's face it: some ideas will fail, these are the facts, and it is simple statistics. Sometimes failures inspire new ideas for things that do work. It is a process and as long as you don't jump into anything too expensive that would affect your overall business, it is always worth the try. Just remember: small steps.

Yes, change is the one constant and it couldn't be any more true or obvious than it is in the world we live in today. It took 75 years for 100 million people to adopt the telephone, and it only took several years for Facebook to become the main marketing tool for thousands of businesses, inspiring tens of other social media channels, some of which were just as powerful. So, it's better to embrace the course of positive change and make it your own along the way by learning from our mistakes and challenges.

It is very important to transform every field either in a professional career or in personal life. Every day both a person and the environment we live in, face several challenges and also offer multiple new opportunities. Changes, adjustments, and learning from failures that one encounters are an integral part of a personal development journey and positive factors one learns through failure must be embraced. Change touches all aspects of life and can and can contribute towards positive personal development.

Internal change promotes focus. Change enables one to become the person they want to become and regular practicing and enacting change is one of the most rewarding processes. External change brings dramatic improvements. Internal change promotes encouragement and external change will drive the confidence to push forward. So, growing up with challenges that life throws, is fundamental for healthy personal development.

6 ways to embrace change

Small adjustments to your habits and mindset can break down any resistance to change and welcome the uncertainty that comes with it. Here are six examples of embracing change with inspirational quotes to help you leave your comfort zone.

1. Write it down

"You're never too old to set another goal or to dream a new dream." – C.S. Lewis

When debating a big change, your mind might flood with conflicting emotions, what-if scenarios, and worries. The important part is to get it all out on paper. Once you've written it all down, you can look for patterns or mental blocks you need to overcome to feel safer making a change. close-up-of-man-journaling-at-home-alone-embrace-change.

2. Accept your fears

"When I dare to be powerful, to use my strength in the service of my vision, then it becomes less and less important whether I am afraid." – Audre Lord

You can fight off many fears by fostering a positive mindset. Consider whether boosting your confidence might help you notice and leverage your strengths to feel more prepared for the unknown.

3. Hire a coach

"If you don't like something, change it. If you can't change it, change your attitude." – Maya Angelou

Successful people understand that life isn't a solo journey. Leaning into your community of friends, colleagues, and mentors provides the moral support you need to believe in yourself. Working with a professional coach is another great way to gain effective support.

4. Embrace creative thinking

"A man who views the world the same at fifty as he did at twenty has wasted thirty years of life." – Muhammad Ali

Creativity promotes greater resilience by teaching you to be flexible and resourceful. Consider taking a pottery class, joining a reading group, or sketching your surroundings to promote creativity daily. Whatever activity you take up, curiosity will lead to success in other areas of life, like cultivating a better work-life balance and enforcing new boundaries in relationships.

5. Share with others

"It is not the strongest of the species that survive, nor the most intelligent, but the one most responsive to change." – Charles Darwin

Being a part of a supportive social network can reduce stress and improve well-being on your self-improvement journey. Whether embracing change in the workplace or your personal life, turning to your support network can help you feel accompanied and encouraged to flip to the next chapter of your life. And when you bring others into your journey, you become a leader of change, passing the potential for positive transformation around.

6. Consult with a mental health professional

"When you come out of the storm, you won't be the same person who walked in. That's what the storm is all about." – Haruki Murakami

When fear or worries become too loud to hear yourself think, it may be your signal to seek help from a mental health professional. your distress and resistance to change.

Learn to love change. When you embrace change, whether subtle or significant, you invest in your personal growth and fulfillment. While it may be hard work, recognizing your values, setting clear goals, and bringing your community on board will help transform change from an obstacle to a catalyst for self-betterment.